Belfast Studies in Language, Culture and Politics

General Editors: John M. Kirk and Dónall P. Ó Baoill

1:    *Language and Politics: Northern Ireland, the Republic of Ireland, and Scotland*
      published 2000 ISBN 0 85389 791 3

2:    *Language Links: the Languages of Scotland and Ireland*
      published 2001 ISBN 0 85389 795 6

3:    *Linguistic Politics: Language Policies for Northern Ireland, the Republic of Ireland, and Scotland*
      published 2001 ISBN 0 85389 815 4

4:    *Travellers and their Language*
      published 2002 ISBN 0 85389 832 4

5:    Simone Zwickl, *Language Attitudes, Ethnic Identity and Dialect Use across the Northern Ireland Border: Armagh and Monaghan*
      published 2002 ISBN 0 85389 834 0

6:    *Language Planning and Education: Linguistic Issues in for Northern Ireland, the Republic of Ireland, and Scotland*
      published 2002 ISBN 0 85389 835 9

7:    Edna Longley, Eamonn Hughes and Des O'Rawe (eds.) *Ireland (Ulster) Scotland: Concepts, Contexts, Comparisons*
      published 2003 ISBN 0 85389 844 8

8:    Maolcholaim Scott and Roíse Ní Bhaoill (eds.) *Gaelic-Medium Education Provision: Northern Ireland, the Republic of Ireland, Scotland and the Isle of Man*
      published 2003 ISBN 0 85389 847 2

9:    Dónall Ó Riagáin (ed.) *Language and Law in Northern Ireland*
      published 2003 ISBN 0 85389 848 0

10:   *Towards our Goals in Broadcasting, the Press, the Performing Arts and the Economy: Minority Languages in Northern Ireland, the Republic of Ireland, and Scotland*
      published 2003 ISBN 0 85389 856 1

12:   Shane Murphy, Neal Alexander and Anne Oakman (eds.) *To the Other Shore: Cross-Currents in Irish and Scottish Studies*
      published 2004 ISBN 0 85389 863 4

Doonsin' Emerauds:

New Scrieves anent Scots an Gaelic / New Studies in Scots and Gaelic

Edited by J. Derrick McClure

Cló Ollscoil na Banríona
Belfast 2004

First published in 2004
Cló Ollscoil na Banríona
Queen's University Belfast
Belfast, BT7 1NN

Belfast Studies in Language, Culture and Politics
www.bslcp.com

Doonsin' Emerauds is taken from Hugh MacDiarmid's poem "Gairmscoile", I:
   ... And there's forgotten shibboleths o' the Scots
   Ha'e keys to senses lockit to us yet
   — Coorse words that shamble thro' oor minds like stots,
   Syne turn on's muckle een wi' doonsin' emerauds lit.

-

British Library Cataloguing-in-Publication Data
A catalogue record for this book is available from the British Library.

ISBN 0 85389 860 X

Typeset by John Kirk in Times New Roman

Cover design by Colin Young
Printing by Optech, Belfast

CONTENTS

The papers in this volume were first presented at the **Seventh International Conference on the Languages of Scotland and Ulster**, which was organised by the Forum for Research on the Languages of Scotland and Ulster, and was held from 6-9 August 2003 at the Crichton Campus, Dumfries, of the University of Glasgow.

CONTRIBUTORS

Dr. Andrew Breeze, a graduate of the Universitities of Oxford and Cambridge, has taught since 1987 at the University of Navarre, Pamplona. Married with six children, he is author of more than 300 research papers and of the controversial study *Medieval Welsh Literature* (Dublin, 1997), and co-author with Professor Richard Coates of *Celtic Voices, English Places* (Stamford, 2000).

Dr. Sheila Douglas, who was born in Yorkshire and grew up in Renfrew, graduated in English from the University of Glasgow. She published much of the material collected for her University of Stirling PhD as *The King o the Black Art and other folk tales* (Aberdeen University Press 1987). More of her research on Travellers appeared in *Scottish Language* (14/15, 1995-96) and *Travellers and their Language* (Cló Ollscoil na Banríona, 2002). From 1971-88, she taught English at Perth Academy and from 1997-2003 was Scots Language Tutor on the BASM course at the Royal Scottish Academy of Music and Drama, where she still does seminars on the History of Scottish Music and helps on the Folklore Course. She has also worked on the editorial team of the *Greig-Duncan Folksong Collection*. Sheila is one of Scotland's leading traditional singers, and a collection of her own songs was published as *Lines upon the Water* (Ossian Publications, 1997). Sheila is a tireless campaigner for the recognition of Scots in all its varieties. With a view to promoting Scots better in schools, she has founded with her sons the Merlin Press, which produces Scots teaching resource material. She has published a children's novel called *The Magic Chanter* (Scottish Children's Press 1997) and has written two more children's novels, an historical novel set in Georgian Perth, and a biography of Gavin Greig's great grandson, Arthur Argo, each looking for a publisher. She is currently working on a book about Traveller tradition bearer, Willie MacPhee.

Gavin Falconer is a Parliamentary Reporter at the Houses of the Oireachtas in Dublin and was previously Sub-editor (English and Ulster-Scots) at the Northern Ireland Assembly. He is working on the *Basic Scots Bible* with Dr. Ross G. Arthur of York University, Toronto. A native of Milngavie, he studied German and Irish Studies at the University of Liverpool, and was subsequently awarded a PGCE by Queen's University Belfast, where he is now engaged in postgraduate research on Scots.

J. Derrick McClure was born and brought up in Ayr and is a graduate of Glasgow and Edinburgh Universities. He is a Senior Lecturer in the Department of English, University of Aberdeen. His published works include *Why Scots Matters* (Saltire Society Publications, 1988 and 1997), *Scots and its Literature* (Benjamins, Amsterdam, 1995), *Scotland o Gael an Lawlander, a volume of Scots translations from contemporary Gaelic poetry* (Gairm Publications, Glasgow, 1996), *Language, Poetry and Nationhood* (Tuckwell, Edinburgh, 2000), *Doric: the Dialect of North-East Scotland* (Benjamins, Amsterdam, 2002) and over sixty articles on Scottish linguistic and literary topics in various journals, festschrifts and conference proceedings volumes. He is Chairman of the Forum for Research on the Languages of Scotland and Ulster, and editor of the annual journal *Scottish Language*. In 2002 he was awarded an MBE for services to Scottish culture.

Dr. Kenneth MacKinnon is Visiting Professor and Emeritus Reader in the Sociology of Language at the University of Hertfordshire, Honorary Fellow in Celtic at the University of Edinburgh, and an Associate Lecturer in Social Sciences, Education and Language Studies of the Open University. From 2000-2002, he was a member of the Ministerial Advisory Group on Gaelic (MAGOG) and in January 2004 was appointed a director of the Scottish Executive's Gaelic Language Board. He is internationally known for his work in demo- and ethno-linguistics, and language planning and development. His research interests include a focus on Celtic language groups, in particular Gaelic and Cornish.

Sandra Mhairi McRae is currently working towards a PhD in sociolinguistics at the University of Aberdeen. Having conducted an introductory study into the changing roles of demonstrative forms within a speech community in Aberdeenshire at undergraduate level, she has spent three years expanding this research question. This has included an examination of the linguistic ecology of the area in tandem with fieldwork conducted in the Burgh of Inverurie focusing on language variation and change. Her introductory study is summarised in an article in *Scottish Language* no.19 (2000): 'The Demonstrative Pronouns in the North-East: an introductory discussion'.

Dr. Colin Milton is Associate Director of the Elphinstone Institute at Aberdeen University. The remit of the Institute, which he helped to set up, is to record, study and promote the vernacular culture of North-East and North Scotland. Dr Milton currently teaches in the ethnology and folklore MLitt offered by the Institute, and researches the history of nineteenth and twentieth century Scottish literature. He has published on poetry in Scots from the nineteenth century vernacular revival to the Scottish Renaissance of the twentieth century; on the portrayal of the Great War in Scots poetry; on Tom Leonard's use of urban Scots, and on the links between local traditions of verse and song-making and the 'national' literary tradition. He is currently writing on Margaret Oliphant, George MacDonald, R M Ballantyne and Arthur Conan Doyle for the forthcoming *Edinburgh History of Scottish Literature*.

Dr. Robert McColl Millar lectures in Linguistics at the University of Aberdeen. He has published on the interface between Gaelic and Scots in Northern Scots, lexical attrition in Modern Scots, rapid language change and its connection with language contact, the development of the definite article in English and language attitudes in modern Scotland. His first book, *System Collapse, System Rebirth: The Demonstrative Systems of English 900-1350 and the Birth of the Definite Article*, was published by Peter Lang in 2000. His second, *Language, Power and Nation*, will be published by Palgrave Macmillan in late 2004. He is the co-ordinator of the Language and Identities in the North-East of Scotland initiative.

Dr. Michael Montgomery is a native of Tennessee and is Distinguished Professor Emeritus of English at the University of South Carolina, where he remains an active researcher on the English and Scots of Scotland, Ulster, and the United States and on trans-Atlantic connections between them. Among the offices he currently holds are President of the American Dialect Society, Honorary President of the Ulster-Scots Language Society and Honorary President of the Forum for Research on the Languages of Scotland and Ulster. He has edited three books on Ulster Scots and eight on the English of the American South, including his historical dictionary of Appalachian English (University of Tennessee Press, March 2004).

Caoimhín Ó Donnaíle [Kevin Donnelly] was born in Dublin, brought up in Ayr, studied mathematics, physics, statistics and mathematical genetics before turning increasingly to computing, and learned Irish Gaelic, Scottish Gaelic and a smattering of Manx and Welsh. For the past twelve years he has been the head of computing at the Gaelic-medium college Sabhal Mor Ostaig in Skye, and is the author of the bulk of its extensive website. He has placed online several Gaelic dictionaries together with the college's *Stòr-dàta Briathrachais Gàidhlig* ('Gaelic terminology database'), incorporating versatile search facilities. He serves on the committee for the UK indigenous minority language corpus project at Lancaster University.

Roz Smith lectured for the last quarter of the twentieth century at the Caledonian University in her native city of Glasgow. She knows a variety of European languages, and her interests include Celtic philology. She is now retired and enjoying foreign travel, while keeping a close eye on linguistic developments in the various dialects of Scotland.

Introduction

J. Derrick McClure

The Seventh International Conference on the Languages of Scotland and Ulster, organised by the Forum for Research on the Languages of Scotland and Ulster, was held from 6-9 August 2003, at the Crichton Campus of the University of Glasgow. Following the precedent of the fourth conference in the series, at Sabhal Mòr Ostaig, the location was not a major university centre but a seat of learning chosen for the appropriateness of its location: Dumfries, with its Burns associations and place in the heartland of a vigorous and distinctive dialect of Scots, and proximity also to Northern Ireland.

The conference, though attracting fewer participants than its immediate predecessors, fully maintained the tradition of academic excellence and social conviviality which has become a hallmark of the series. Delegates visiting from the Irish Republic, Spain, Germany, Norway, the United States and Japan, as well as Scotland and Ulster, enjoyed the fine setting and excellent hospitality of the Crichton Campus. A bus excursion to local places of interest is an invariable feature of these conferences, and this one proved a memorable event as on previous occasions: among other things, delegates were regaled with *Tam o' Shanter* at Ellisland farm and *The Dream of the Rood*, both in the original Anglo-Saxon and in Tom Scott's imposing Scots translation, in the church housing the Ruthwell Cross.

The ten papers in the present volume,[1] which include the four plenaries, confirm that the academic standard of the conference series was fully maintained: that is, it represented the leading edge of research in dialectology, sociolinguistics, toponymics and folk studies as applied to the ever-changing language situations in Scotland and Ulster. **Robert Millar** sets the field of Scottish linguistic studies in a wider context by comparing the long-term language conflict in North-East Scotland with similar but more complex situations in Western and Eastern Europe. Andrew Breeze ranges as widely in time as Millar in space with his examination of some of Scotland's oldest place names, not only for their meaning but for the light they cast on linguistic and demographic history. **Kenneth McKinnon's** topic, by contrast, is urgently contemporary: the condition of Gaelic as revealed by the most recent census figures; and the still-critical state of the language is forcefully demonstrated by his findings. An ongoing project is described by **Caoimhin Ó Donnaile**, showing that notwithstanding the struggles of Gaelic as a

---

[1] The previous six conferences are published as follows:
1. Aberdeen, 1985: *Scottish Language*, 5, 1986
2. Glasgow, 1988: *Gaelic and Scots in Harmony,* ed. Derick S. Thomson. University of Glasgow: Department of Celtic, n.d. [1988]
3. Edinburgh, 1991: *Studies in Scots and Gaelic,* ed. A. Fenton and D.A. MacDonald. Edinburgh: Canongate Academic, 1994
4. Sabhal Mòr Ostaig, 1994: *Scottish Language,* 14/15, 1995-96
5. Aberdeen, 1997: *Scottish Language*, 17, 1998
6. Belfast, 2000: *Language Links: The Languages of Scotland and Ireland.* ed. J.M. Kirk and D.P. Ó Baoill. Belfast: Cló Ollscoil na Banríona, 2001

community language researchers are contributing to the field using the most up-to-date electronic techniques.

The next three papers are on Scots. The field of Scots historical research is represented by **Michael Montgomery's** article, in which a corpus of sixteenth- and seventeenth-century letters is examined for evidence of the ongoing loss of distinctively Scots features of orthography and grammar. **Sandra McRae** discusses her own investigation of a distinctive local feature of a North-Eastern dialect; and the difficulties both practical and theoretical of developing Scots (Ulster Scots, but the arguments could be applied in Scotland as well) in its utilitarian and non-literary register are explored in depth and detail by **Gavin Falconer**.

Finally, three papers focus on — by a broad definition — literary topics. **Colin Milton**, discussing the Greig-Duncan folk-song collection, takes issue with several entrenched assumptions regarding the status of both folk-song and the language which is its medium; and **Sheila Douglas** draws interesting observations from her own experiences as a collector and singer of traditional Scottish song. The entertaining essay by **Roz Smith** demonstrates in detail that Scottish newspapers, contrary to what might be assumed, make lively and revealing use of not only the indigenous languages of Scotland but others too.

Several papers presented at the conference are not included here: some are likely to be published elsewhere as given; the material discussed in others will eventually be incorporated in reports on projects as yet incomplete.[2] Nonetheless, this collection not only illustrates the wide range of topics and high quality of discussion which characterised this conference but forms an important contribution to the ever-growing corpus of published research on the languages of Scotland and Ulster.

---

[2] Papers not included in the present volume:

Barbara Bird (University of Oslo), 'Under the Influence? Looking for Patterns of Change in Western Isles English Pronunciation'.

Marion Gunn (University College Dublin), 'A Scottish Language and Three Lexicographers'.

John M. Kirk (Queen's University Belfast), 'The Irish Component of the International Corpus of English', to appear in A. Renouf and A.Kehoe (eds.) *The Changing Face of Corpus Linguistics* (Amsterdam: Rodopi, 2004).

Caroline Macafee (University of Aberdeen), 'The History of Scots to 1700: Something Old, Something New'.

Morag MacNeil (University of Edinburgh), 'Gaelic-Medium Teachers: Initial Education and Continuing Professional Development'.

J. Derrick McClure (University of Aberdeen), 'A Local Treasure-Trove: John MacTaggart's', to appear in the *Transactions of the Dumfriesshire and Galloway Natural History and Antiquarian Society*, 78, 2004.

Roibeard Ó Maolalaigh (University of Edinburgh), 'On the Possible Connection between Scottish Gaelic *iorram* and Scots *yirm*', to appear in Michel Byrne, Thomas Owen Clancy and Sheila M. Kidd (eds.) *Rannsachadh na Gàidhlig 2*, University of Glasgow.

Rab Wilson, 'The Cormilligan Sonnets'.

Linguistic History on the Margins of the Germanic-speaking World: Some Preliminary Thoughts

Robert McColl Millar

1. Introduction

Until the achievement of the European Union in recent years, most of us had a clear idea of what a *border* represented. It was the place where the national – or rather the state – apparatus was at its most visible; it was the place where the greatest power was exercised upon the individual, whether native or foreign, by representatives of a polity, a point discussed at length by Anderson (1996). Even today, crossing a border can have a powerful linguistic impact. If we pass from, say, France to Italy, we decisively leave one linguistic state for another in official terms, despite the fact that historically there was a dialect continuum running across the territory. Within a country, this state apparatus is less visible, unless the traditions or laws of that polity are flouted. This is a very different situation from the border in the past (in many places, the very recent past). The closer you approached the centre of a state/nation/polity, the greater the play of power would be. In many places, the borders of polities were hazy and, in a very real sense, *marginal* in a variety of ways. As a number of cultural anthropologists, such as Sahlins (1989) and Donnan and Wilson (1999) have demonstrated since the breakthroughs by Barth in 1969, identity on the margins is different from social and personal identity in the centre of a polity.

In the first place, it is more fluid. Historically, identity in marginal regions has been capable of flux, depending on technology and clothing; on occasion, even hairstyle, as suggested by Bartlett (1993) and Ascherson (1995). At its heart was the use of language as an identifier of social identity. To use an area outside the present focus of this paper: the reason why rules on the use of English language, dress and tradition among the Old English in Ireland, such as the statutes of Kilkenny of 1367, were so draconian and detailed was precisely because there was slippage between identities: quite natural, in fact, on the margins, but confusing and unsettling to those whose linguistic and cultural identity was more settled and less situational. In essence, marginal regions increase cultural *hybridity*, often expressed in terms of language as well as tradition. A particularly telling recent example of this can be seen analysed in Bulag (1998) in relation to the means by which an individual defines himself as Mongolian or Chinese in Inner Mongolia. The 'mongrel' identity (as perceived by those who inhabit the linguistic-cultural centre, particularly since the Romantic period) can also be construed as a positive hybrid which is capable of reinterpretation by an individual according to the domains s/he inhabits.

What happens, therefore, when this hybridity on the margins comes into contact (and therefore conflict) with the developing state-apparatus of the modern nation, as defined by Anderson (1983), among others? From our point of view, what linguistic effects can this tension between identities and polities produce? In order to illustrate these questions, I wish to present a comparative preliminary discussion of three areas on the margins of the Germanic world where there is (or has been) contact with members of another subfamily of Indo-European – the Ardennes-Eifel region, the former provinces of East and West Prussia, and the North of Scotland. Can we see similarities between the linguistic development of these ostensibly very different regions? Can discussion of one region lead to a deeper understanding of developments in another?

2.1 The Ardennes-Eifel region[1]

The Ardennes-Eifel area is a study in contrasts. Culturally the area is relatively homogenous, associated primarily with a combination of arable and dairy farming, with heavy industry to be found on its fringes. Throughout the region similarities of cuisine and lifestyle abound. Historically it was one of the final heartlands of Celtic-speaking Gaul, before being conquered by the Franks. Yet linguistically the region today is strikingly diverse, a factor which is recognised to some degree by the fact that an area significantly smaller than Scotland is divided among five countries. What is equally striking is the awareness, even after a brief exposure to the area, that the linguistic situation as it stands at present cannot represent or explain the linguistic patterns of the past.

There are a number of oppositions at work in this territory. In the first place, there is the major distinction between the Romance and Germanic languages which at first glance follows the boundary between the Belgian legislative area of Wallonia and the French province of Lorraine, and the rest of the region. Within the Germanic area a generally recognised distinction would be made between German and Dutch, as well as a less generally recognised distinction between Luxembourgish and Standard High German. From an administrative point of view, these distinctions follow national and provincial frontiers very neatly. Yet if we look more closely we can see that this neatness is illusory.

In the first place, the absolute distinction between Romance and Germanic is not so. There are pockets of Germanic speech in Wallonia and Lorraine; and of Romance speech in Luxembourg, a point much discussed by historians of the Frankish conquest, such as Joris (1965) and James (1988), in terms of *why* the linguistic frontier should have fallen in places where it has no topographical significance. Historically, a number of towns which are completely Germanic in language now – Maastricht, Prüm, Trier, among others – had significant Romance speaking populations. How these populations are treated in relation to the majority language of their specific area depends very much on both national and local political conditions and the histories of the various sub-regions of the Ardennes. In Northern Lorraine, towns such as Thionville (and, historically, Metz) had (and to some extent still have) significant numbers of German/Luxembourgish speakers, but, in line with the unitary pieties of the French state, have little in the way of provision for their Germanic speakers; in Belgium, Germanic-speaking inhabitants of *Neubelgien* – those areas of the former kingdom of Prussia which were incorporated into Belgium as part of the provisions of the Treaty of Versailles in 1919 – have considerable local and provincial linguistic rights, with the

---

[1] A great deal of the information underlying this section has been derived from Kloss (1978), Berg (1993), Gilles (1998), Barbour and Carmichael (2000), Hogan-Brun (2000) and Treffers-Dalton (2002). Many of the conclusions derived are mine, however.

exception of the Malmédy area: a special case, as we will see. In *Altbelgien*, however, those historically Germanic-speaking areas (with the exception of Dutch-speaking Flanders, naturally) which have been incorporated in Belgium since 1830, little in the way of linguistic rights is available to the local non-Romance populations, even when, as in the case of Arel/Arlon, a majority of the population were at least historically German/Luxembourgish speaking. Finally, there is the *Voerstreek*, a small part of the Liège area of historically Dutch-speaking population (or, rather, Germanic, but not German, -speaking population, since the question of language-assignation is part of the problem of the area). Historically, this area was part of the *Land van Overmaas*, a territory of mixed language now split politically between Belgium, the Netherlands and the Federal Republic of Germany. Although having a boundary with the officially Dutch-using Belgian territory of Flanders might make it seem sensible for it to pass over from Wallonia, precisely this transfer has been debated quite violently since the 1950s at least, primarily because many Dutch-speakers in the area feel strong historical, cultural, perhaps even emotional, ties with Liège.

Contemporary Luxembourg is a perplexing combination of trilingual and monolingual nation. The official language of the nation is Standard French; the national language is *Lëtzebuergesch* – Luxembourgish – a Moselle Franconian dialect of Middle German with decided interference from French (including Walloon) at a variety of levels – lexical, phonological and to some extent structural – of the linguistic system. Since the 1970s, what Heinz Kloss described (1978: 104-116) as a *Halbsprache* has gradually assumed more and more of the characteristic features and functions of a full-blown *Ausbau* language. German has a strangely shadowy existence within the Grand-Duchy: it has quasi-official rather than actual official status, but occupies a considerable space in the media and governmental domains. With the exception of many of the large numbers of Portuguese migrants to the country, whose preferred mode of external communication is, quite understandably, French, the overwhelming majority of Luxembourgers use Luxembourgish as their preferred means of communication, at least orally. The one exception to this is a small group of communes on the border between Luxembourg and Belgium in the neighbourhood of Klierf/Clervaux and Bastogne/Basternach who use a Romance dialect in their day-to-day communication. There is some evidence that despite (or perhaps because of) the overwhelming presence of Standard French in Luxembourg, these communities are switching to Luxembourgish.

In the Ardennes-Eifel areas of the Federal Republic of Germany and the Netherlands, only limited domain space is given to any other linguistic usage except the standard varieties of High German and Dutch.

Yet this pattern of standard languages associated with a given state, and small-scale linguistic minorities living within the linguistic universes of the majority populations, with differing rights depending on the state involved, is only part of the story. In both the contemporary Romance and Germanic areas of the region the language varieties employed are (or were) generally highly divergent from their perceived standard varieties.

The 'French' spoken in the Ardennes is defined by some language activists as a separate Romance vernacular, Walloon. It is highly divergent at all levels of the system and, in its most dense form, is not readily intelligible with other varieties of 'French'. Having said that, the great majority of Romance speakers in the area no longer speak this variety in its 'purest' form. Instead, a continuum exists between dialect and standard, along which many speakers regularly travel. To a lesser extent, but in an analogous way, language attitudes in French-speaking Belgium are reminiscent of those held in France, as discussed by Balibar (1985); in fact, many Belgians have attempted to lose even their 'Walloon' accent, as well as elements of specifically Belgian French, such as the loss of distinction between simple and perfective aspect in the past tense, which may demonstrate either an areal Ardennes feature, or perhaps even a substratum Germanic interference. Although there have been attempts afoot to preserve Walloon and to develop a standard orthographical system, this seems a somewhat forlorn hope. There is one exception to this, however. In the Malmédy region, Walloon as both a living spoken and to some degree written language is in far better health. Strikingly, this region is a relatively recent incorporation into Belgium (1919); prior to this, Malmédy had never formed part of any French-speaking polity. Under Prussia (and its predecessors), Malmédy had been dominated since the process of vernacularisation and mass education began by standard High German. Knowledge of standard French was extremely limited, particularly since the valley in which the town stands was surrounded by majority German-speaking territories in the shape of Eupen and St Vith. Although market towns such as Liège and Spa are not a great distance away, political pressure and sheer physical ease would have made it less problematical to trade in German-speaking towns. There is also some evidence that the Prussian authorities actively encouraged the use of Walloon in order to downplay potential Belgian irredentism. Some of this sense of separateness has survived in the region, although the domains previously dominated by German have naturally been taken over by standard French since the Versailles settlement.

On the Germanic side of the divide, the actual linguistic situation is as complex, if not more so. Those minority populations in France and Belgium who live close to the border of Luxembourg tend to speak similar Moselle Franconian dialects (in other words rather northerly Middle German dialects which form part of the 'Rhenish Fan' in terms of their level of adherence to the Second Germanic Consonant Shift). More northerly varieties of 'German' in Belgium are also Middle German, shading gradually into dialects which share much in common with both Dutch and Low German (or rather with the 'Low' varieties of Germanic historically spoken in contiguous areas of what is now the Federal Republic of Germany and the Netherlands). They all incorporate significant degrees of French influence in their spoken forms. There are striking differences between the use favoured in *Neubelgien* and elsewhere. In those areas which were historically part of Luxembourg, and in particular Arel/Arlon, there seems to be an awareness of, and pride in, the distinctiveness of the local variety, of its connection with Luxembourg, and of its difference from standard German. There is considerable tolerance of, perhaps even admiration for, the French language. In *Neubelgien*, however, the local varieties are rarely seen in writing; instead, standard High German is emphasised in all public domains. French is barely tolerated; ritual defacement of bilingual road signs is common. Indeed, the linguistic distance between these areas and their contiguous officially German areas is slight.

Although historically Germany has been deeply tolerant of local dialects and their use in the spoken sphere (a tolerance which, as Leopold [1968] points out, may now be wearing thin), standard High German is omnipresent. To the east of France, Luxembourg and Belgium, the French influence upon the local dialects peters out fairly quickly, although there is some evidence for its having been greater in the past, before the area's induction into larger (and more aggressively 'German') conglomerations took place. There is considerable evidence for a shift along a continuum towards the standard.

In the Netherlands province of Limburg, there is some evidence of French influence upon the local Frankish dialect, a dialect which in many ways shares more in common typologically with the Northern Middle German dialects than it does with standard Dutch. Again, however, standard Dutch is omnipresent, and there is considerable evidence of new contact varieties developing along a continuum between southern Limburgs and Dutch (Kloss 1978: 203-204).

Luxembourg marks itself off from these situations by the fact that the local set of dialects has managed both to maintain itself and increase its prestige. Potential reasons for this distinctiveness will be suggested later in this paper.

2.2 East and West Prussia

The historical linguistic ecology of the two former provinces of West and East Prussia is fraught with problems. In the first place, the interchanges of population between the Soviet Union, Poland and Germany in the aftermath of the Second World War, with accompanying renaming of many places, both big and small, and if not that, the 'loss' of one or more of a set of names for a particular place in the process, has altered utterly the linguistic status of the area in question: the north-west provinces of Poland and the Kaliningrad *oblast'* of the Russian Federation, appear monolingual and monocultural; moreover, the suspicion, when reading history stemming from this bitter period, is that this has always been the case. This is only the last of a series of effacements in the modern era, however. The Baltic and Slavonic basis of Prussia was largely and conveniently ignored during some periods of German language hegemony, in particular those associated with the second German Empire and the Third Reich. No territory is free from the ideological bias of its rulers; the former provinces of Prussia have suffered the consequences of these prejudices in spades.

Yet this was not always the case. It suits (and has suited) modern nationalist historiography on all sides to express the relationship between the various linguistic and ethnic-cultural groups which inhabit and inhabited these regions as being ones of conflict and exclusivity. Certainly there have been periods when this has been the case; as striking, at least until the modern period, has been the level of hybridity which has been possible in these border regions. As a brief aside, inspired by the work of Norman Davies (1981: I, 150-152, 257; II, 25-26), we can observe a figure such as the astronomer we know as Nicholas Copernicus. In his own lifetime, Copernicus was a hybrid figure (and, in that sense, by no means unusual for the period: it is merely his achievements and their lasting effects which make him stand out). He was a subject of the King of Poland from his city of Thorn-Torun. There is little doubt that he came from a German-speaking family, at least in recent years, (although it is more than likely that his Pomerelian/Prussian Low German would have been incomprehensible to most speakers of what we think of as German, both then and now). He was, it should be noted, an implacable critic of the Hohenzollern Dukes of Prussia, who ruled from Königsberg. There is considerable evidence that he could read, write and speak Polish, even if his writings were largely in Latin. Yet this mixed nature has been in recent years almost impossible to accept for either Polish or German historians. Indeed, modern hybrids such as Günter Grass are often treated less as products of their mixed environments than as heretics linguistically and culturally.

Whereas with the Ardennes-Eifel region the environment of valley-based communes lent itself to the preservation of local varieties of speech along with a strong sense of peasant individualism and large-scale local autonomy, this could not be the case in what became the Prussian provinces. In the first place, the area lies in the low-lying North-European plain, and is dissected by three major river systems – the Odra, Vistula and Niemen. Its coastline is famous for its large salt lagoons, called *Haff* in German, *zalew* in Polish. The province of East Prussia, the most desolate part of the region, was historically covered by coniferous forest. The point of this geographical excursus is that the area is relatively easy to conquer, but difficult to defend and control for any length of time. Ninteenth-century German historiographers often referred to Poland as a *Saisonstaat*, a 'seasonal state'. In fact, as the subsequent history of the Prussian state demonstrates, this is true for all modern or pre-modern polities which have attempted to control the region.

The early cultural and linguistic history of Prussia is largely legendary, with occasional insights from external observers and by place-name evidence, as described by Carsten (1954) and Schmalstieg (1976). There is some reason to suspect that speakers of East Germanic languages passed through what became West Prussia in the early years of the Common Era. Although much was made of this presence by German ideologues in the nineteenth and twentieth centuries, lack of proximity to the literate world means that we do not have the evidence for their settlement which we do for the long-term survival of a Gothic presence in, for instance, the Crimea. When Wulfstan of Hedeby made his voyage to the eastern Baltic reported to King Alfred and produced as an addendum to the Old English translation of Orosius' *History against the Pagans*, the division between what became West and East Prussia was already notionally present, with apparently Slavonic-speaking peoples living west of the Vistula, apparently Baltic-speaking peoples living to the east. This is the position apparently maintained in the High Middle Ages, when German speakers first become involved in matters pertaining to the Baltic shore.

As Bartlett (1993) demonstrates, the experience of German speakers east of the Elbe has been one of long-term settlement beside people who spoke other languages, and whose presence in the territory in question has generally been of greater duration. In the nineteenth century it was fashionable to think of these movements, generally described as the *Drang nach Osten*, the 'push towards the East', as being in part a civilising mission, in part an actual displacement of peoples, rendering the areas in question (which happened to be the heart of the new expansive German state) German in civilisation and 'race'. Even at the time, this view was difficult to maintain. The further east one travelled in 'Germany' along the Baltic shore, the more it was the case that speakers of other languages were present. Certainly it is true that some of these varieties – such as the Slavonic

Polabian or the Baltic Prussian – did die out in the early Modern era; much more was maintained, however, a fact that can be seen in the contemporary survival of Sorbian. Yet it was not, of course, the speakers of these languages who died out; merely (if it can be termed such) their languages. It was not only Germanic dialects which were expanding at this time as well. There is considerable evidence that West Slav language varieties were also expanding in what was to become East Prussia at the expense of Baltic varieties (whether defined as Prussian or Lithuanian), East Slav varieties (later defined as Belarusyn) and even Germanic varieties. The situation is complex, hybrid and mutually stimulating.

The nature of what was meant by nationality at the time has to be interrogated, in fact. There is little doubt that there was a perception among many inhabitants of the region that being 'German' or 'Polish' brought with it certain advantages, particularly in cultural and technological terms. Yet these categories were fluid; it was certainly possible to represent yourself by a variety of identities depending on place and time.

All of this hybridity was also fed by the nature of the evolving understanding of social roles – and particularly of the status of nobility – in the area. Whilst the nobility of 'Poland' were never as linguistically diverse as was the case in the comparable Kingdom of Hungary, it is certainly true that for long periods of time the estate-based vision of society encouraged a sense of commonality between people of different linguistic backgrounds, in particular in the noble estate. Indeed, the fact that, east of the Odra, occupational function often defined language (and therefore cultural identity) cannot be ignored. 'Germans' worked the land in particular ways, traded in certain ways, even ate and dressed in certain ways; so did 'Slavs'. Naturally, this was not an equal situation: social dominance led to political dominance on the part of German speakers, with the concomitant spread of the German language as the default language. That does not make the linguistic ecology of Prussia at the end of the Middle Ages monolithic, however.

It is also worth noting that the Germanic and Slavonic varieties spoken in the region were divergent in a number of ways from the 'national', standardised languages which were beginning to develop closer to the centre of the developing nations. Indeed, the Low German of cities like Danzig-Gdansk was of considerable prestige throughout the Baltic, remnants of which can be seen in its effects on practically every other language spoken in the area, as evidenced by a number of papers in Ureland (1987).[2] At the same time, remnants of Baltic speech were to be found, particularly in the neighbourhood of Memel-Klajpeda and the backwoods of East Prussia. The Slavonic dialects of West Prussia were (and are) deeply divergent from those of central areas of Poland, to the extent that many scholars (although few of them Polish) would be inclined to define them as representing a separate language, Kashubian (Kloss 1978: 25). All of these language varieties influenced each other; Kashubian and Low German in particular were given literate expression. Regularly, inhabitants of the area would have spoken more than one of these varieties. There is some evidence from both that period and later that people may have assigned different identities to

---

[2] There is also some evidence for the influence of Slavonic dialects on Germanic ones on this set of borders, as shown by evidence for the former Grand-Duchy of Auschwitz, collected by Wicherkiewicz (2003).

themselves depending on the language they were speaking at the time.

This hybridity also spread to matters of religion. In the early modern period many Slavonic speakers became Protestants, albeit generally Calvinists in distinction to the Lutheranism favoured by many speakers of the Germanic varieties. By the same token, many speakers of these Germanic varieties, in particular those from a peasant background, maintained their Catholic identity. The Kingdom of Poland was, and remained, extremely tolerant of a variety of religious persuasions within its bounds. The tradition of Polish obscurantism is, to put it mildly, somewhat exaggerated. Nevertheless, it is true to say that the gradual reconversion of the majority of Polish-speaking Protestants to Catholicism (strangely, it has been suggested, not due to persecution but, in fact, the lack thereof) as well as the alteration in power-relationships in the region, with Prussia combining with overwhelmingly German Brandenburg, sloughing off its allegiance to the Polish state, and, indeed, becoming an aggressor power in relation to Poland, led to a greater concentration on the association of linguistic identity with religious and ethnocultural identity.

This binarity can also be seen in language. As Wells (1985: 310) points out, although Kings in (later, Kings of) Prussia maintained elements of Low German in their private writings well into the eighteenth century, and this was probably normal across the literate population of Prussia, there is no doubt that the prestige of High German, as the language of Church and State, led to its gradual conquest of a variety of the domains originally associated with the local variety. The same was largely true of the local Slavonic varieties, which gradually came under the influence of the standard emanating from the Polish centre, perhaps even more treasured as the Polish state collapsed. There were exceptions to this, however, largely due to the inclusion of large Slavonic minorities within Prussia (even before the annexation of actual 'Polish' territories such as Poznań-Posen).

As well as the speakers of Kashubian, whose largely Catholic identity and large-scale bilingualism in Low German rendered their identity highly hybrid, depending on the functional domain, the presence of large numbers of Slavs of Protestant confession in the Elbląg-Elbling and Olstyń-Allenstein regions of southern East Prussia led to a gradual 'severing of the ties' between the local varieties and 'mainstream' Polish. German scholars often talk of a language named *masurisch* – Mazurian (Kloss 1978: 24). In these areas, public life (including to a very large extent church life) would have been carried out in (High) German; pride in the local variety, distinct and divorced from Polish, was nonetheless maintained. Elements of these identity combinations made their presence felt in the twentieth century, when a significant part of the Mazurian population voted to remain part of Germany rather than join the new Polish Second Republic (Davies 1981: II, 401).

Although much of this hybridity has been lost since 1945, I will return again to Kashubian identity towards the end of the paper. Before I do so I would like to turn to a discussion of a marginal territory which represents a linguistic rather than a political boundary.

2.3 Northern Scotland

At first glance it might seem that there is significantly less to say about the North of Scotland than about the areas already covered. In the first place, the dynamic of modern inter-state rivalries and synergies is absent from this area. Since the early Middle Ages, the North of Scotland has been a part of a unitary state encompassing areas which are different from it in terms of language, culture, and tradition. Nor can we talk in terms of religion being for any length of time a marker of ethnic identity. Yet there are also similarities between the Ardennes, the Prussias and the North. The North of Scotland is, I would argue, an archetypal border region in many senses.

In the first instance, the geography of the area is illustrative when taken into consideration with the linguistic situation, past and present. With the exception of the Cossiemounth from Stonehaven to Aberdeen, there is no easy way to get from north to south. Transit from east to west or west to east is only really possible in a limited number of areas, most notably the Strathspey and Great Glen valleys. Elsewhere, communication by land was limited until very recently to relatively small distances, while sea travel was much easier. Taking the North-East as an example of this, we can see that, as Horsburgh (1997) has illustrated, the historical linguistic ecology of the region has been carried out largely in relation to itself, with little or no reference to elsewhere (with the exception perhaps of the area around Dufftown/Glenlivet). Its primary linguistic influence outside of this region has been either along the south shore of the Moray Firth or in 'leaps' across to the Black Isle and Caithness, among other areas. The languages involved in this process have changed; not the process itself, however. Nevertheless, it can be seen, with a very broad interpretation of the terminology, as a form of colonisation of one language (and culture) by another over a long period of time. In the first place, Pictish is gradually replaced by Gaelic; later, due at least in part to the power struggle between the House of Moray and its southern rivals during the eleventh century, and definitely due to the ongoing Normanisation of the country which can be interpreted as a form of plantation in this area, Gaelic hegemony was gradually replaced by that of an increasingly localised variety of Scots.

If we examine Caithness for a moment we can see this: we can assume, I think, that there was a Pictish presence in this area, but that there were also Gaelic speakers present before the Norse invasions. Place-name evidence would suggest that the more fertile east and north of the territory were primarily settled by speakers of Norse dialects, whilst the west remained Celtic in speech (Nicolaisen 1982). We have little in the way of records for what Caithness Norse looked like, but it is very likely to have had more Celtic features than the equivalent varieties in Orkney and in particular Shetland. It perhaps would not have become as Gaelicised as Manx Norse appears to have become, however: primarily because of the presence of neighbouring (and prestigious) varieties of the language to the North. With the gradual 'Scottish' takeover of power in the region, the similarities between Norse and Scots would have led to a relatively straightforward changeover from one to the other – particularly when the same process began to be played out in the Orkneys as well.

In a sense we have here a process which has been found in Scotland and elsewhere at a variety of time periods. The urban areas and the large farms are 'colonised' by speakers of a language variety close to that of the centre. The 'border' lies between these settlers and those both with less economic power and holdings in more marginal areas. Widespread (although probably not entirely mutual) bilingualism probably existed; indeed, Caithness speech today demonstrates just such a level of interference between Gaelic and Scots – and quite possibly the Norse which preceded it – in its use of, for instance, *this* and *that* with plural nouns and in its preference for /f/ over /ʍ / (Black 2003). These may be importations from the North-East, but it is striking that their presence is felt in an area where similar phenomena would also be present. This is particularly the case when there is such a high incidence of Gaelic vocabulary in the local dialect (Richard 2003).

On the fringes of this Celtic territory, therefore, we can assume a set of 'borderland' areas where two languages and, to some extent, cultures, came into contact with each other: the North-East; the Black Isle; the Dornoch area; Caithness. The linguistic ecology of each of these areas was and is different from the others; yet they also shared much in common. In each, 'marginal' varieties of both the 'colonising' and 'colonised' languages developed, different from more 'mainstream' varieties of either language. These varieties interacted with each other, even if they were in competition with each other. There is every reason to imagine, in fact, that a status-based form of diglossia was present from a relatively early period, as I have demonstrated in evidence from the early eighteenth century of the linguistic ecology of the Formartine area of Aberdeenshire (Millar 1996). Certainly, the higher status of Scots led to its preference over time among those who wished to 'get on'; this was a slow process, however. Indeed, if this process had been permitted to develop without interference from elsewhere, it is very likely that this diglossic situation could have been maintained.

As we all know, however, this did not happen. A sense must have been present from the fifteenth century on among literate members of the Scots-speaking community that certain varieties of Scots – those approaching metropolitan norms, in fact – were preferable to that spoken in their area; a fact demonstrated by the very small amount of evidence we have for usage which, it might be assumed, dates from an early period. Over time, of course, this sense of superiority was reinforced by the use of the exonormic Standard English, a set of developments discussed by Devitt (1989) and Meurman-Solin (1993), among others. In some ways this acted as a protection (and encouragement) to the local variety, of course, since the distance between the local variety and the metropolitan norm became significantly greater; in a unitary state where a premium was placed on literacy in the standard variety, however, this divergence would inevitably come to resemble a double-edged sword.

In fact, elements of this can be seen in the way in which, beyond a certain point which can be related largely to date, English replaced Scots as the language of prestige in marginal Gaelic areas. A very good example of this can be seen in upper Deeside. As a number of scholars have pointed out – most recently Middleton (2001) – a line passes through the Deeside area just to the west of Logie Coldstone beyond which the Scots is significantly less dense than it is to the east. The Scots found there is also not as obviously North-Eastern in phonology and lexis as it is elsewhere in the region. This area was, of course, Gaelic-speaking until at least the eighteenth century and, in pockets, into living memory. In this area, it was English as taught in schools which was the primary language in the changeover to a Germanic variety. Yet Scots elements prevailed to quite a remarkable degree in these new varieties: largely, it might be assumed, through a desire to be associated with group (perhaps even national) identity. Similar phenomena are observable in a number of areas across which the language boundary between Gaelic and English/Scots has passed during periods of literacy, such as Nairn or Inverness; indeed, it can perhaps be seen in recent years, in places such as Stornoway. Yet where this has happened, the variety of Scots used does not demonstrate all of the features of the parent dialect, as a comparison of the dialects of the Moray Firth area seems to demonstrate.

On the Gaelic side, the situation remained fairly stable until the 'improvement' movement of the eighteenth century. Outside the burghs, in the marginal lands, Gaelic was retained to a high degree. To be sure, the middle classes would have been bilingual in English and the local variety; furthermore, the high level of temporary migration to the Lowlands found throughout the Highlands and Islands would have allowed for a considerable knowledge of both local and distant varieties of Scots (a point made often in, for instance, the first *Statistical Account of Scotland*, where the language 'mixing' involved is commented upon in a disapproving manner, as discussed in Millar 2003). Nevertheless, this facility with language would have been situational.

As Dorian's seminal study of 1981 demonstrated, the human effects of agricultural improvement led to disruptions in this situational model, with, eventually, Gaelic being associated with a particular trade which declined, taking the language with it. Naturally, the particular ecology of the Dornoch area – the history and identity of the Sutherland family, for instance – may have been a contributing factor in the speed with which Gaelic declined among the native (rather than transplanted) peasantry during the 'clearances'; nevertheless, it can be assumed that the dislocation caused by improvement and its associated educational and ecclesiastical impulses in the late eighteenth and nineteenth centuries along the linguistic margin would have led to a shift in the balance between the two linguistic entities, disastrous to Gaelic, very unlike anything which had come before. In a sense, although the process took place in the modern age, the fate of Gaelic on the margins resembles those of earlier languages, such as Prussian or the Belgic Celtic dialects which had no external or internal state/national support in competition with languages which had such support. The difference is that the power of the state (rather than the nation) has increased exponentially since the eighteenth century, so the process is quicker, more extensive, and more visible. In the process (on both sides) hybridity is lost.

3. Conclusions

I would therefore suggest a number of conclusions which can be derived from these case studies:

First, geographical inaccessibility and marginality has led to the survival of lesser-used languages into relatively recent times. This marginality has led to the development of varieties of all languages concerned which express hybridity. Naturally, power differentials may have led to this being expressed at different levels of the linguistic structure. For instance, Prussian Low German may show a small degree of Slavonic interference, generally at the level of lexis, as suggested by Damme (1987); this is nothing compared with the influence Low German (and to some extent High German) has had on Kashubian and Mazurian. By the same token, the mainstream French used in Belgium and Lorraine demonstrates little or no influence from the Germanic languages; it is worth noting, however, that the Walloon of Malmédy, where German was until relatively recent times dominant, demonstrates just such levels of interference. The Germanic dialects of the Ardennes-Eifel reflect the influence of French largely depending on political allegiance – which may actually tell us something. There is considerable evidence to suggest that French influence upon 'German' was all-pervasive for a considerable distance inside what is now Germany proper. As we might expect, we see similar phenomena in the North of Scotland. There are some Celtic influences upon Scots as a whole, and there might be some evidence for more of such influence in the North – indeed I would argue that this is very much the case – but it is surprisingly limited, as Macafee and Ó Baoill (1997) have pointed out. There is considerable evidence from the eighteenth century, when the relationship between the two languages was still relatively static, of Scots influence upon Gaelic. It can, in fact, be demonstrated that there were hybrid dialects on the ground on this margin, and that the more prestigious variety gradually was stripped of these features.

Second, with the advent of the modern nation state during the eighteenth and nineteenth centuries, two processes became predominant. In the first place, the marginal variety which could not be seen as related to the standard variety of the nation became increasingly excluded both from public discourse and also within families. Thus Arel/Arlon, formerly largely Germanic in speech, became increasingly French due to pressures to conform to the Belgian state (particularly easy to carry out in this Luxembourg area, because of the high status accorded to French). This 'move to the centre' was particularly prevalent when ideology came into play. Although the process was interrupted by the end of the Second World War, there is considerable evidence that Protestant speakers of Mazurian were shifting to German in East Prussia.

Third, speakers of the 'marginal' variety which could be identified as an 'aberrant' version of the national variety itself came under increasing pressure in a period of growing literacy to conform to the national norms. This can be seen in the gradual demotion of the western varieties of 'German', the southern varieties of 'Dutch' and the eastern varieties of 'French' found in the Ardennes region. It can be seen in the ways in which the Scots and Gaelic of the contact zones in the North have come under considerable stress to conform (particularly poignant in the case of Gaelic, where the whole language community is under stress to conform to an entirely external norm, yet distinctions of this sort can be seen in the treatment of East Sutherland Gaelic-speaking children by their Western Isles Gaelic speaking teachers, as discussed by Dorian [1981: 80-84]). Specifically Prussian varieties of Low German gradually lost their status. In that region, given the shifting frontiers after the Second World War, particularly unfortunate forces were brought to bear upon Kashubian as well. As Gwiazda (1994) and Majewicz (1996) have pointed out, with the inclusion of the entirety of what had been West Prussia into the Polish state in the aftermath of this war, the hybrid nature of Kashubian culture was problematised. Ironically, their unique variety had actually been partially protected by their largely Catholic enclave identity in a majority German-speaking, Protestant state. Kashubian people did not need to address the difference between Kashubian identity and Polish identity. From 1945 on, the

Catholic identity of Poland could now be equated with Kashubian identity, in a state which wished to stress the 'Polish' identity of the 'recovered territories' as well as the 'Polishness' of what was really an alien regime,[3] and was furthermore encouraging large-scale settlement of eastern Poles (from what is now Belarus and Ukraine) into the area. It was only with the advent of the Fourth Polish Republic in the late 1980s that Kashubian identity and language could once more be discussed (and even taught) in the Gdansk area.

The exception to this process of homogenisation is Luxembourg, where, for reasons which are probably *not* linguistic or cultural in origin, a nation state developed which eventually employed its hybrid identity as a marker of national identity. In a sense, this 'middle way' was only really possible in an area where the tensions between two regional powers – France and Germany – led to the development of a 'neutral zone'.

What does stand out as a difference between Northern Scotland and all the other areas discussed in this paper is the status of Gaelic. In pre-modern times, there was little difference between the margin of Scots and Gaelic and the other margins; in modern times, Gaelic had no nation state to retreat into, unlike all of the other situations discussed here. Certainly, much of the hybrid nature of the borderlands has been lost in most of these areas, but survival of a national, standardised, variety of the language has been practically guaranteed. This is not the case for Gaelic, with disastrous consequences not only for the marginal varieties, but for the language as a whole.

In many ways, this paper leaves more unsaid than said; indeed, it was for that reason that I used the term *preliminary* to describe it. What is certain is that the processes discussed can be traced in, and some of the conclusions applied to, a number of other situations in Europe. Given the nature of the conference at which this paper was initially presented, I am more than aware of questions which could be raised in the discussion of marginality and hybridity in Ireland, and in particular Ulster. Elsewhere on the Germanic margin, it would be fascinating to discuss areas such as southern Finland, Silesia, the former Austrian province of Carniola, the Tyrol and Alsace (discussed in part by Gardner-Chloros 1991). Other margins, both past and present, must be fruitful for linguistic and sociolinguistic analysis: Transylvania, Volhynia, Macedonia, Granada, Brittany, to name just a few. Studies of this type, combining history and linguistic ecology, along with anthropology, are only beginning.

---

[3] A point made by Janicki and Jaworski 1993 in relation to the 'first congress' of the Polish language held in the mid 1980s in Sczeczin, apparently as a means to shore up the then military-political dictatorship.

References

Anderson, Benedict. 1983. *Imagined Communities. Reflections on the Origin and Spread of Nationalism.* London: Verso.

Anderson, Malcolm. 1996. *Frontiers: territory and state formation in the modern world.* Cambridge: Polity.

Ascherson, Neal. 1995. *Black Sea.* London: Cape.

Baldwin, John R. (ed.) 1982. *Caithness. A Cultural Crossroads.* Edinburgh: Scottish Society for Northern Studies and Edina Press.

Balibar, Renée. 1985. *L'institution du français. Essai sur le colinguisme des carolingiens à la république.* Paris: Presses Universitaires de France.

Barbour, Stephen and Catherine Carmichael (eds.) 2000. *Language and nationalism in Europe.* Oxford: Oxford University Press.

Bartlett, Robert. 1993. *The making of Europe: conquest, colonization and cultural change 950-1350.* London: Lane.

Barth, Fredrik (ed.) 1969. *Ethnic Groups and Boundaries. The Social Organization of Culture Difference.* Bergen and Oslo: Universitetsforlaget.

Berg, Guy. 1993. *>> Mir wëlle bleiwe, wat mir sin<<: Soziolinguistische und sprachtypologische Betrachtungen zur luxemburgischen Mehrsprachigkeit.* Tübingen: Niemeyer.

Black, Diane. 2003. The Demonstrative Pronouns in Caithness: a Sociolinguistic Study. Unpublished MA dissertation, University of Aberdeen.

Bulag, Uradyn E. 1998. *Nationalism and Hybridity in Mongolia.* Oxford: Clarendon Press.

Carsten, F.L. 1954. *The Origins of Prussia.* Oxford: Clarendon Press.

Davies, Norman. 1981. *God's Playground: a history of Poland.* 2 vols. Oxford: Clarendon Press.

Damme, Robert. 1987. 'Westslavische Reliktwörter im Stralsunder Vokabular'. In Ureland 1987: 163-178

Devitt, A.J. 1989. *Standardizing Written English: Diffusion in the Case of Scotland 1520-1659.* Cambridge: Cambridge University Press.

Donnan, Hastings and Thomas M. Wilson. 1999. *Borders: Frontiers of Identity, Nation and State.* Oxford and New York: Berg.

Dorian, Nancy C. 1981. *Language death: the life cycle of a Scottish Gaelic dialect.* Philadelphia: University of Pennsylvania Press.

Fishman, Joshua (ed.) 1968. *Readings in the Sociology of Language.* The Hague and Paris: Mouton.

Fishman, Joshua (ed.) 1993. *The Earliest Stage of Language Planning. The "First Congress" Phenomenon.* Contributions to the Sociology of Language 65. Berlin and New York: Mouton de Gruyter.

Gardner-Chloros, Penelope. 1991. *Language Selection and Switching in Strasbourg.* Oxford: Clarendon Press.

Gilles, Peter. 1998. 'Virtual Convergence and Dialect Levelling in Luxembourgish'. *Folia Linguistica* 32: 69-82.

Gwiazda, A. 1994. 'Poland's Policy towards its National Minorities'. *Nationalities Papers* 22: 435-44.

Hogan-Brun, Gabrielle (ed.). 2000. *National Varieties of German outside Germany.* German Linguistic and Cultural Studies 8. Bern: Peter Lang.

Horsburgh, David Henry Robert. 1997. Gaelic language and culture in north-east Scotland: a diachronic study. Unpublished PhD dissertation, University of Aberdeen.

James, Edward. 1988. *The Franks.* Oxford: Blackwell.

Janicki, Karol and Adam Jaworski. 1993. 'Language purism and propaganda: The First Congress for Polish'. In Fishman 1993: 219-32.

Joris, André. 1966. 'On the Edge of Two Worlds in the Heart of the New Empire: the Romance Regions of Northern Gaul during the Merovingian Period'. *Studies in Medieval and Renaissance History* 3: 1-52.

Kloss, Heinz. 1978. *Die Entwicklung neuer germanischer Kultursprachen seit 1800.* 2nd edn. Düsseldorf: Schwann.

Leopold, Werner F. 1968. 'The Decline of German Dialects'. In Fishman 1968: 340-364.

Macafee, C.I. and Colm Ó Baoill. 1997. 'Why Scots is not a Celtic English'. In Tristram 1997: 245-286.

Majewicz, A.E. 1996. 'Kashubian Choices, Kashubian Prospects: A Minorty Language Situation in Northern Poland'. *International Journal of the Sociology of Language* 120: 39-53.

Meurman-Solin, Anneli. 1993. *Variation and Change in Early Scottish Prose: Studies Based on the Helsinki Corpus of Older Scots.* Helsinki: Suomalainen Tiedeakatemia.

Middleton, Sheena Booth. 2001. A Study into the Knowledge and Use of Scots amongst Primary Pupils on Upper Deeside. Unpublished MLitt dissertation, University of Aberdeen.

Millar, Robert McColl. 1996. Gaelic-influenced Scots in pre-revolutionary Maryland. In Ureland and Clarkson 1996: 387-410.

Millar, Robert McColl. 2003 '"Blind attachment to inveterate customs". Language Use, Language Attitude and the Rhetoric of Improvement in the first *Statistical Account*'. In Dossena and Jones 2003: 311-330.

Nicolaisen, W.F.H. 1982. 'Scandinavians and Celts in Caithness: The Place-Name Evidence'. In Baldwin (1982): 75-85.

Richard, Jan. 2003. Investigating Lexical Change in Caithness. Unpublished MA dissertation, University of Aberdeen.

Sahlins, Peter. 1989. *Boundaries: the making of France and Spain in the Pyrenees.* Berkeley: University of California Press.

Schmalstieg, William R. 1976. *Studies in Old Prussian.* University Park and London: The Pennsylvania State University Press.

Treffers-Dalton, Jeanine and Roland Willeyms (eds.) 2002. *Language Contact at the Romance-Germanic Language Border.* Clevedon: Multilingual Matters.

Tristram, Hildegard L.C. (ed.) 1997. *The Celtic Englishes.* Heidelberg: C. Winter.

Ureland, P. Sture (ed.) 1987. *Sprachkontakt in der Hanse. Aspekte des Sprachausgleichs im Ostsee- und Nordseeraum. Akten des 7. Internationalen Symposions über Sprachkontakt in Europa, Lübeck 1986.* Tübingen: Max Niemeyer.

Ureland, P. Sture and Iain Clarkson (eds.) 1996. *Language contact across the North Atlantic.* Tübingen: Max Niemeyer.

Wells, C.J. 1985. *German: a linguistic history to 1945.* Oxford: Clarendon Press.

Wicherkiewicz, Tomasz. 2003. *The Making of a Language. The Case of the Idiom of Wilamowice, Southern Poland.* Berlin and New York: Mouton De Gruyter.

Scottish Place-Names: The Way Ahead

Andrew Breeze

Introduction

Nothing is more Scottish than a Scottish place-name; and it is cheering that this aspect of Scotland's identity is now gaining more attention than ever. The Scottish Place-Name Society has been issuing its newsletters (since 1996) and holding its conferences; Professor Wilhelm Nicolaisen's *Scottish Place-Names* has reached its latest edition (in 2001); and Dr Simon Taylor of St Andrews, Dr Carole Hough of Glasgow, and others are publishing important research. The way for discoveries is rapidly opening up. So now is a good moment to look forward and see what finds can be expected, what techniques are likeliest to produce them, and what pitfalls should be avoided.

Everyone knows that Scotland's place-names are of mixed origins. We have to deal with English, French, Norse, Gaelic, Cumbric, and Pictish forms, while some of the oldest and most obscure names are no doubt pre-Celtic and pre-Indo-European. What follows comments on toponyms of Brittonic origin (both Pictish and Cumbric), as this is the author's special area of knowledge. Such an approach has two advantages. It can explain toponyms from some of the earliest records we have for Scotland, dating from Roman times and hence before the arrival of Gaelic in the fifth century. It also shows what can be explained by reference to Welsh, the living language closest to the extinct Cumbric and Pictish of medieval Scotland. Our understanding of the Brittonic languages has been revolutionized by the work of Sir Ifor Williams (1881-1965) and *Geiriadur Prifysgol Cymru* (1950-2002), which does for Welsh what *A Dictionary of the Older Scottish Tongue* and *The Scottish National Dictionary* have done for Scots. But the implications of this for Scotland's past will take time to work out. We are here very far from the evening of our labours.

What follows discusses eleven Scottish place-names under four headings. The places referred to are: (a) *Abravannus, Graupius, Verubium Promontorium* (**Noss Head**, Caithness), and *Virvedrum Promontorium* (**Duncansby Head**); (b) **Arran, Cumnock, Girvan**, and **Irvine**; (c) **Loquhariot**; and (d) **Pennango** and **Soutra**. The first group contains forms from Roman times; the second, some names of Cumbric origin; the third casts light on early Christianity in North Britain; and the last two have Arthurian links. So there should be something here for all interests.

Noss Head, Piltanton Burn, Bennachie, and Duncansby Head

(a) *Abravannus, Graupius, Verubium Promontorium*, and *Virvedrum Promontorium*. These are four puzzling forms from Roman Britain. The second (which, through a medieval printing error, gives modern 'Grampian') occurs in the work of Tacitus, describing the final conflict of Agricola and the Caledonians. The others occur in the *Geography* of Ptolemy, writing in second-century Alexandria. *Abravannus* has been described as of unknown meaning, but identified with the river Luce, near Stranraer. The second has been corrected to *Craupius*, of unknown meaning, and identified with **Bennachie**, Aberdeenshire. As for the two headlands in Caithness, the third has been dubiously explained as 'very pointed cape', the fourth as 'very wet cape'. This is not very satisfactory.

Now, *Abravannus* will be a British form; the other three are presumably Pictish, which may here be regarded (following the authority of Professor Kenneth Jackson) as very similar to British. What happens if we try to explain all four by comparison with Welsh? If we do this, some surprising things happen. First, *Abravannus* would give Welsh *Afrwan, which would mean 'very weak one'. This makes no sense for a torrent like the Luce. But it makes good sense for the Luce's sluggish western neighbour Piltanton Burn, flowing through flatlands to the south of Stranraer. It seems Ptolemy's *Abravannus* can be identified as this stream, especially as recent coin-finds (now in Stranraer Museum) point to the existence of Roman beach-markets by its estuary. So we may reasonably conclude that Ptolemy's *Abravannus* is **Piltanton Burn** (NX 1156) and means 'very weak one, very feeble one'.[1]

Now for Tacitus's (emended) *Craupius Mons*. Following the discovery of a Roman Camp at Durno (NJ 6927), Aberdeenshire, this has been taken as **Bennachie**, a mountain dominating the Aberdeenshire countryside for miles around. But no meaning has been extracted from the form. However, the existence of Welsh *crib* 'comb; crest (of a bird); top, summit, ridge (of a hill)' allows a drastic but possible emendation of *Craupius* to *Cripius 'comb; cock's crest'. This would make excellent sense as a name for **Bennachie**, which is a long-ridged mountain with four distinct peaks. Comparison with medieval Celtic languages thus lets us emend Tacitus's *Graupius Mons* to *Cripius Mons* 'comb hill, cock's-comb hill', and take it as **Bennachie**, which had a British hill-fort on its summit at Mither Tap (NJ 6822).[2]

Third, *Verubium Promontorium*. This must be **Noss Head**.[3] But the interpretation 'very pointed cape' is philologically weak. Welsh forms suggest another solution. There we have a word *gorudd* 'reddish, bloody'. In the seventh-century *Gododdin* the champion Tudfwlch, whose 'bloodstained blades' covered the ground with corpses, is lamented as a hero 'red (*guorut*) in his fury'. *Gorudd* is also a modern name of the farmland weed Red Bartsia (*Odontites verna*).[4] **Noss Head** is made up of red sandstone, so the form would be an apt one, especially for mariners. An emended *Verudium Promontorium* can therefore be understood as 'very red cape', the ancient name of **Noss Head** (ND 3855), near Wick, Caithness.

As for Ptolemy's *Virvedrum Promontorium*, this is surely **Duncansby Head**, by John o' Groat's House. But the translation 'very wet cape' makes poor sense.[5] Early Welsh *gweir* 'bend' instead allows an interpretation 'very sharp cape', which

---

[1] A. L. F. Rivet and Colin Smith, *The Place-Names of Roman Britain* (London, 1979), 240; A. C. Breeze, 'Abravannus', *Transactions of the Dumfriesshire and Galloway Natural History and Antiquarian Society*, lxxv (2001), 151-2.
[2] Rivet and Smith, 370-1; A. C. Breeze, 'Philology on Tacitus's Graupian Hill and Trucculan Harbour', *Proceedings of the Society of Antiquaries of Scotland*, cxxxii (2002), 305-11.
[3] Rivet and Smith, 497.
[4] Geiriadur Prifysgol Cymru (Caerdydd, 1950-2002), 1502; K. H. Jackson, *The Gododdin: The Oldest Scottish Poem* (Edinburgh, 1969), 111.
[5] Rivet and Smith, 507.

is far more intelligible, with **Duncansby Head** representing a 100-degree turn for mariners rounding Britain. Again, early Welsh means we can explain *Virvedrum Promontorium*, now **Duncansby Head** (ND 4173), as 'very sharp cape'.[6]

With this first group, then, comparison with Welsh allows what appear to be corrections of form, location, and meaning, but in the case of **Bennachie** strengthens views arrived at on other, archaeological grounds; so that philology would confirm the opinion that of one of the most famous battles ever fought in Scotland took place below **Bennachie**, Aberdeenshire (and not elsewhere).

Arran, Cumnock, Girvan, and Irvine

The second group, with the names of **Arran**, **Cumnock**, **Girvan**, and **Irvine**, contains forms that can be taken as Cumbric (a language, similar to Welsh, spoken in much of southern Scotland until about the year 1100). Although Gaelic etymologies have persistently been proposed for them, none of these has been convincing. The first now refers to an island, but can be understood by reference to mountain-names in Wales; the others now refer to towns, but seem to derive from the names of rivers.

Once again, if we compare these forms with what can be gathered from early Welsh, some interesting results occur. *Aran* is the name of peaks in North Wales, all similar to the spiky summits of **Arran** which are an unforgettable sight for travellers south-west of Glasgow; *aran* is also a common noun meaning 'spike'. So there is reason to understand **Arran** as having a Brittonic toponym meaning 'spike (island), peak (island)', which would make good sense for this heavily-eroded granite massif with six peaks above 2,500 feet, the highest of them being Goat Fell (NR 9941).[7] In geographical contrast to **Arran** is **Cumnock**, a working town in East Ayrshire. Given the failure of Gaelic etymologies for its name to attract wide support, another approach is suggested by the Welsh word *cymynog* 'hewer, cutter'. A Cumbric equivalent of this might have been a river-name; if so, it would have been that of Carsgailoch Runner, a short but vigorous stream approaching the town from moorland to the south. This has cut a wooded dell for itself into the landscape, as can be seen even from a small-scale map. So there seems reason to take **Cumnock** (NS 5619) as having a Cumbric name (like nearby Ochiltree 'high farm, high settlement'), in this case deriving from the river at its foot.[8] That would have parallels elsewhere in Ayrshire. The town of **Girvan** (NX 1898), where golfers look over the sea to Ailsa Craig, is surely called after the turbulent Water of **Girvan**, a namesake of the Garwin 'rough one', a stream (SN 1828) in the Prescelly Mountains of Dyfed.[9] As for **Irvine** (NS 3238), this ancient burgh and new town is called after its river, itself apparently named after a humble but useful herb, the wild turnip (Welsh *erfin*, Breton *irvin*), a common plant of

---

[6] Richard Coates and Andrew Breeze, *Celtic Voices, English Places* (Stamford, 2000), 79-80.

[7] A. C. Breeze, 'Some Celtic Place-Names of Scotland', *Scottish Language*, xix (2000), 117-34.

[8] A. C. Breeze, 'Cumnock', *Transactions of the Dumfriesshire and Galloway Natural History and Antiquarian Society*, lxxv (2001), 153-5.

[9] A. C. Breeze, 'Some Celtic Place-Names of Scotland', *Scottish Language*, xviii (1999), 34-51.

river banks, which has been cultivated since the New Stone Age as a vegetable rich in oil, and which perhaps gives its name to a burn called Erfin (SN 6983) in the hills east of Aberystwyth.[10] This second group hence shows how comparison with Welsh or Breton may provide solutions for long-standing problems, and even cast light on early Scottish ecology and food supply. It also provides a warning of the dangers of seeking Gaelic etymologies for toponyms in Cumbric parts of Scotland.

Loquhariot

Our third group contains one item. **Loquhariot** (NT 3760), a hamlet eight miles south-west of Edinburgh, is familiar to historians as a centre for the cult of St Kentigern. The Celtic elements in written accounts of him, especially as regards toponyms, were the subject of a classic study by Professor Kenneth Jackson.[11] Yet he gave no explanation for this strange-looking form. However, a solution is indicated by comparison with Welsh, Cornish, and Breton, where the element *loc-* 'cell; shrine' is a familar one, generally followed by the name of the saint who lived or was venerated at a particular spot. As for the rest of this Lothian toponym, an explanation is indicated by the Welsh personal name *Gwrwaret*, which has equivalents in early Cornish and Breton. Their Cumbric equivalent may have been the name of a hermit of the Cumbrian Church, whose cult was based at **Loquhariot**, but whose memory was later all but obliterated by that of the hero of the Cumbrian Church, Kentigern. If this explanation holds water, it shows how a toponym can provide information on the early Christianity of North Britain, of which so little is otherwise known.[12]

Pennango and Soutra

Finally, King Arthur. Many parts of Britain have contended for him. In recent years the subject has even reached the House of Commons, where Scottish MPs (perhaps having in mind the continuing success of Scotland's tourist industry) have called him a North British hero. What follows discusses two toponyms with Arthurian links: **Pennango** near Hawick, and **Soutra**, near Edinburgh.

Let us look first at **Soutra**. This is an old upland parish and viewpoint south of Edinburgh, with the well-known medieval hospital of the Holy Trinity (NT 4558) above the 1200-foot contour. **Soutra** figures in early records as *Soltre*, where the first element is of unclear meaning, but the second one is a Cumbric form meaning 'settlement, farmstead'. There is reason to identify **Soutra** with a place in the eleventh-century *Mabinogion* tale of Culhwch and Olwen. When the hero Culhwch arrives at Arthur's court, the porter says he will raise a shout that will be heard 'in the depths of Dinsol in the North'. The whereabouts of this has puzzled scholars; but there is reason to take it as a *din* or fort by *Soltre* or **Soutra**,

---

[10] A. C. Breeze, 'Irvine', *Transactions of the Dumfriesshire and Galloway Natural History and Antiquarian Society*, lxxv (2001), 155-6.
[11] K. H. Jackson, 'The Sources for the Life of St Kentigern', in *Studies in the Early British Church*, ed. Nora Chadwick (Cambridge, 1958), 273-357.
[12] A. C. Breeze, 'St Kentigern and Loquhariot, Lothian', *Innes Review*, liv (2003), 103-7.

which had strategic importance over millennia. Maps of Roman and medieval Britain bring out the significance of Dere Street, running from the Tyne via Carter Bar and Melrose into Lothian. Armies used this road to invade Scotland or England; the military implications of **Soutra**, where forces from the south would at last see Edinburgh Rock and begin descending to the Lothian plain, are hence obvious, as is shown by remains of a Roman signal fort there (identified in 1976 from air photographs). If **Soutra** is the *Dinsol* of the Arthurian tale of Culhwch and Olwen, it shows that memories of the spot persisted in Wales long after political links between Welsh and Cumbrians were cut in the seventh century.[13]

Last of all, **Pennango** and its possible links with Arthur's battle of *Mons Agned*, attributed to him in the ninth-century *Historia Brittonum*. **Pennango** figures in medieval documents as a spot (now not precisely located) in southern Scotland, apparently near the junction of Teviot and Allan Water (NT 4510) four miles south of Hawick. The first element *pen* 'head, headland' is clearly Cumbric. But what is the second element? Once again, comparison with Welsh suggests a (somewhat sinister) solution. The element here would correspond to *angau* 'death', so that the form would mean 'death headland, death hill'. It is not hard to think of this as a name on an important route (now the A7 trunk road) through steep hills, where attack by bandits would be easy. There are parallels with *Morpeth* 'murder path' in Northumberland or *Dupath* 'thief path' in east Cornwall. But there may be more to it than that. There is slight evidence to identify **Pennango** with *Mons Agned*, the site of one of Arthur's twelve battles according to *Historia Brittonum* (formerly attributed to Nennius). The argument is this. Nobody has ever extracted any meaning from *Agned*. But a simple emendation to *Agued* does provide a meaning, since *agwed* is an archaic Welsh word meaning 'death; strait'. *Mons Agued* would therefore also mean 'death hill', and is sufficiently close to *Pennango* in form, meaning, and possible situation to suggest they may have been the same place.[14]

If so, there would be interesting implications. Whether Arthur actually fought at **Pennango** is unlikely and effectively unprovable (though not totally so, if archaeologists ever turn up fifth-century badges or buckles there, indicating the site of a battle). But it is possible that a ninth-century Welsh chronicler imagined Arthur fought at this spot, not least because another battle in his list, that of the Caledonian Wood, can be located near Beattock (as even Kenneth Jackson accepted), while later recensions of *Historia Brittonum* replace *Mons Agned* with *Breguoin*, almost certainly the present-day High Rochester (NY 8398), Northumberland. That would still leave us in North Britain and would strengthen the case of those like Dr Rachel Bromwich of Cambridge and Kenneth Dark of Reading, who (despite fierce and sustained opposition from Kenneth Jackson) have argued that the earliest evidence for Arthur implies that he was a North British hero. If, then, some wish to see Arthur as a fifth-century leader fighting in the hills around Hawick, there is place-name testimony for this.

---

[13] A. C. Breeze, 'The Names of Bellshill, Carmichael, Lauder, and Soutra', *Innes Review*, li (2000), 72-9

[14] A. C. Breeze, '*Historia Brittonum* and Arthur's Battle of *Mons Agned*', *Northern History*, xl (2003), 167-70

Conclusion

A full understanding of Scotland's place-names requires an understanding of medieval languages possessed by nobody on this planet. The problems of toponymy hence need co-operation between individuals. If that is forthcoming, we shall all be the gainers, whether our interests are in language, archaeology, history, geography, folklore, or even ecology. There is no predicting just what may turn up. With true scientific impartiality, place-name study may locate a palace, a battlefield, or a pig-sty; it may tell us what language the men and women of long ago spoke, what clothes they wore, and what they had for dinner; like the map in *Treasure Island*, it can even be used to locate buried treasure.[15] In short, the implications of place-name research, in Scotland as elsewhere, are almost without limit.

---

[15] See the writer's 'The Battle of the *Uinued* and the River Went, Yorkshire', forthcoming in *Northern History*.

Gaelic in the 2001 Census: A few green shoots amidst the gloom

Kenneth MacKinnon

Gaelic in Scotland's population census

A question on Gaelic has been asked in Scotland's population census since 1881, when 231,602 'habitual speakers' were enumerated. The number rose to 254,594 in 1891 with a question change to 'can speak Gaelic'. Since then numbers have consistently declined with the sole exception of a rise from 80,978 to 88,892 between 1961-71 when questions on reading and writing abilities were asked for the first time. (Figures are as given in successive census Gaelic Reports 1961–91.) The 2001 census carried an additional question for the first time of understanding the language. The total of actual speakers as such had declined to 58, 969, with a further 7,094 persons returned as able to read and/or write but not speak Gaelic, and there were an additional 27,538 persons claiming understanding ability alone.

This rapid overall decline of speakers is reflected in the decline of young people speaking the language. The proportion of speakers aged under 25 has fallen from 26.7% of all Gaelic speakers in 1921 to 21.9% in 2001. A proportion of 33.3% is basic for language maintenance – and we are further from this now than ever. These totals and proportions are illustrated in **Figures 1 and 2**.

Gaelic speakers are increasingly dispersed. In 1881 87.84% of all Gaelic speakers were located in the Gaidhealtachd counties now comprising the Western Isles, Highland and Argyll & Bute council areas. In 2001 this proportion had become 55.55%. **Figures 3 and 4** show the distribution of Gaelic speakers across Scotland. Western Isles was home to 26.8% of all Gaelic speakers – just over 1 in 4, with just over 1 in 2 in the Gaidhealtachd area as a whole. Population movement between 1991 and 2001 had resulted in a 10.5% population loss in Western Isles, with a concomitant loss of 19.6% of its Gaelic speakers. The corresponding figures for Argyll & Bute were 0.7% population loss and 14.7% Gaelic-speaker loss. However, Highland gained 2.4% in population with a loss of 18.0% of its Gaelic speakers. Clearly the strongest areas for Gaelic are areas with the greatest economic and demographic problems at the present time – and present policies are insufficient to maintain the language group in sheer numerical terms.

Gaelic speakers by age: 1991 and 2001

The analysis of Gaelic speakers by age indicates very clearly the effect of Gaelic-medium education in increasing numbers of speakers, especially in the 5-11 age group. This indeed shows an advance on the situation in 1991. However, Gaelic-medium policies are quite insufficiently carried though at secondary stage, and this potential growth point can be seen rapidly to fall away in the ensuing 12–15 and 16–19 age-groups. Amongst younger adults of parenting age up to 49 years of age, substantial decline in numbers over the ten-year period is very evident. The present day scale of Gaelic-medium education and its virtual confinement to the primary stage are unlikely to halt or reverse long-standing language-shift even in the so-called 'heartlands' – let alone nationally.

Figure 6 indicates proportions of the total age-group able to speak, read, write and understand Gaelic. Illustrated this way, it is clearly evident that gains from Gaelic-medium education are, from a societal or national viewpoint, very much a case of being merely a small 'blip on the chart'. From the point of view of their significance within the Gaelic language-group in proportional terms, the gains as illustrated in **Figure 7** look more promising – but again it is patently obvious that they are not followed through at secondary or further levels. The age-profiles in both illustrations bear witness to rapid and consistent language-shift throughout the 20th Century.

Reversing language-shift

In January 2003 Bòrd na Gàidhlig was created as a language-planning authority for Gaelic. Its first priority must surely be to address the problems of rapid and catastrophic language-shift and its reversal. The concept has not to date been very adequately or precisely operationalised in demographic terms. The population census gives us a means of assessing and evaluating these processes. Basically language-shift is evident when the numbers or proportions of speakers amongst the generation of childhood is less than that amongst the generation of parenthood. This paper introduces two measures of these processes: firstly, intergenerational gain / loss; and secondly, intergenerational ratio, both of which can enable evaluation and assessment to be derived from census data.

Intergenerational gain / loss is based upon comparison of census data for the 5–15 and 20–44 age groups in the Scottish population census of 2001. These age-groups are to some extent arbitrary but have been constrained by the categories of census theme table T27 where they are thus aggregated. (The categories could be better calculated from standard table S206 when this becomes available for all areas; and similarly for the Welsh standard table S133 and theme table T15) The 5–15 age-group is moreover the age-group of statutory school attendance. The measure depends upon the comparison of proportions of Gaelic speakers within the total populations of each age-group. Where the proportion is greater (e.g. in %-point terms) amongst 5–15s than amongst 20–44s, intergenerational gain is thus indicated, and reversing language-shift may be said to have occurred. Where the proportion is smaller, intergenerational loss is indicated and language shift has occurred.

This measure may be affected by population movements both of Gaelic speakers and – more especially – of non-Gaelic-speakers. A more reliable measure may be found in intergenerational ratio. This compares the actual numbers of speakers of both age-groups. A mean value in terms of single year of age is calculated for each age-group, and then compared as a ratio of the mean of 5–15s divided by the mean of 20–44s. Values above unity indicate reversal of language-shift, and values less than unity indicate that language-shift has been operative. For given areas and census years the values of both measures may be plotted graphically on the Y- and X- axes of a two-dimensional graph. **Figure 8** illustrates this for Scottish council areas in the 2001 census. There were six cases only of intergenerational gain: Argyll & Bute (+3.80 %-points), Highland (+2.45), Stirling (+1.64), Perth & Kinross (+0.83), Clackmannanshire (+0.51), and North Lanarkshire (+0.05). All other cases represented losses. The greatest was Western

Isles (-2.98 %-points).

For intergenerational ratio the positive cases comprised the same six council areas: Stirling (2.91), Argyll & Bute (2.48), Perth & Kinross (2.07), Clackmannanshire (1.96), Highland (1.57) and North Lanarkshire (1.05). In all other cases, the Gaelic-speaking parental generations had failed to reproduce themselves. Just failing to do so were: Western Isles with a ratio of 0.99. The weakest case on this measure was South Ayrshire with a ratio of 0.21. Such lowland local authority areas have not been conventionally regarded as having anything very much to do with Gaelic – but as this study has demonstrated they are home to almost half (44.45%) of all Scotland's Gaelic speakers.

Comparison with Wales

Wales and the Welsh language provide striking contrasts with Gaelic in these particular respects. Between 1991 and 2001 the number of Welsh speakers increased from 508,098 to 582, 368 – a 14.17% increase. This increase was strongest amongst 3–15s, whose numbers had consistently increased since the 1971 census from 77,560 to 83,000, to 113,236, and to 184,407 in 2001 (comprising 36.7% of the total age-group.) In contrast total numbers of Gaelic speakers declined from 65,987 to 58,969. The situation is illustrated graphically in **Figure 9.** Gaelic speakers aged 3–15 declined overall from 9,991 in 1971 to 9,454, to 7,092, with a slight upturn in 2001 of 7,435 (comprising 0.9% of the total age-group.). This situation is illustrated graphically in **Figure 10.**

The calculation of corresponding intergenerational data for Welsh cannot be strictly comparable with Gaelic since the categories for the Welsh data are not exactly the same: 3–15 in the case of the generation of childhood, and 16–44 in the case of the parental generation. These are the categories of the only table so far published to give age data for local authority areas, S137. However, the order of magnitude of the differences in intergenerational processes is so contrastive that these category differences are not very significant. This is obvious from the axis values of the graphs in **Figures 8 and 11**.

All Welsh local authority areas registered substantial intergenerational gains; especially in the more anglicised southeast where the gain was in the order of between 27.3 to 33.7 %-points. In some of the most strongly Welsh areas of northwest and southwest Wales the gain was relatively less (between 12.1 to 14.5 %-points) – as in such areas there is in fact less scope or leeway to make up. Their numerical gains in this respect were nevertheless quite substantial. These results are indicated on the map in **Figure 12**.

The results in terms of intergenerational ratio are perhaps even more dramatic, and area patterns are even clearer. In southeastern Wales, the parental generation multiplied itself between 6 and 9 times in the generation of childhood. Again, in the 'heartland' or 'Bro Gymraeg' areas of western and northwest Wales, the ratios were more modest: between 1.09 and 1.35 in numerical terms. It must be remembered however that these are still substantial gains in situations where there is not the same amount of scope within which to increase them. The situation is illustrated on the map in **Figure 13**.

The situation in the family is illustrated in **Figure 14.** Some 79.18% of families in Wales comprised two non-Welsh-speaking parents, with 28.03% of their children speaking Welsh. Some 9.40% of families in Wales had one Welsh-speaking parent, with 61.10% of their children speaking Welsh. In the case of single or lone Welsh-speaking parents, comprising 2.79% of all cases, 74.74% of their children spoke Welsh. In the case of families with two Welsh-speaking parents (6.69% of all cases), 90.94% of their children spoke Welsh. All other cases comprised 1.94% of all families, with 71.90% of their children speaking Welsh.

Comparable data on Gaelic-speaking parents and their children were not available in August 2003; but in 1991 it was the case that one Welsh-speaking parent was marginally better at imparting the language than were two Gaelic-speaking parents. The weakness of Gaelic family transmission is illustrated in **Figures 15 and 16**, which represent results in the most strongly Gaelic speaking 'heartland' of the Western Isles and of the rest of Scotland in the 1994/95 Euromosaic Survey, with 130 and 192 Gaelic-speaking respondents respectively.

Conclusions

In the case of the results of the 2001 Census for Gaelic language, a few 'green shoots' are quite definitely discernable:-
- Rates of decline have almost halved (52.6%) from an average annual net loss of speakers of 1,333 to 701.
- There were a few local examples of successful intergenerational transmission – but insufficient to reverse language-shift overall. The six 'successful' council areas did not include the principal 'heartland' of the Western Isles.
- Gaelic-medium education had produced some growth – which was not followed through at the secondary stage or beyond. It is not at anywhere near the scale necessary for successful reversal of long-term language-shift.
- The Gaelic 'heartlands' were, and still are, in a state of economic and demographic crisis, with outflow especially of Gaelic-speakers and their dispersal across Scotland and beyond. There was, and continues to be, a significant influx of non-Gaelic-speaking incomers not only for retirement purposes but also to take key jobs and positions.
- Present policies have been failing to maintain the language group in total numbers and especially amongst children and young adults.

Implications

These concerns must be of urgent concern to the recently appointed language authority, Bòrd na Gàidhlig. They are of immediate concern to a local initiative in the Western Isles: the Western Isles Language Plan, which is supported by the local authority Comhairle nan Eilean Siar, the language development agency Comunn na Gàidhlig, the broadcasting funding agency Comataidh Craolaidh Gàidhlig, and based at Lews Castle College, a constituent institution of the University of the Highlands and Islands Millennium Institute.

The position of Gaelic is crucial within the family and community. If Gaelic is to survive as an everyday spoken language these are the priority areas. **Figures 15 and 16** indicate just how weak the position of Gaelic is within the family in even its strongest areas. However, we do not know what turns people on to using the language in these domains, and what turns them off. If there are to be any effective new policies developed by local and national language planners – by local authorities and by Bòrd na Gàidhlig – research is needed to find this out. Very little such psycholinguistic or attitudinal research has so far been attempted in a Gaelic context. Outmoded nineteenth century ideas still inform public opinion and official policy-making, such as: utilitarian philosophy and associated arguments from numbers, the mind as vessel which cannot hold English if it is filled with Gaelic, natural selection, the survival of the fittest, endangered species, clocks ticking to midnight, and patients on life-support systems. The promotion of new attitudes, philosophies, images and policies is long overdue. These could well be based on civil and language rights, Gaelic-speakers as wealth creators and tax-payers, cultural opportunities, creation of conditions for growth, and bilingualism as normal in a Scotland that is part of a globalising, multilingual world.

The use of the term 'heartlands' should imply that the language is taken seriously as a language of education, and that (as in such areas in Wales) children coming into school with whichever language should be enabled to have education and language development both within their home language and within the other language of their community. Such a policy would ensure that at the end of the education process all 'heartland' children would be effectively bilingual. Gaelic-medium education is essentially a means to support the language in non-Gaelic situations. The 'heartland' areas might demonstrate their 'heartland' character by their effective bilingual educational practice throughout the school experience at both primary and secondary levels for all their children.

The Scottish Executive is due to present a draft bill giving 'secure status' to the Gaelic language early in October 2003. If its provisions are to be effective, they will need to be national; otherwise the 3 in 4 Gaelic speakers outwith the Western Isles and the 1 in 2 Gaelic speakers outwith the Gaidhealtachd area will fail to be affected, and the decline of Gaelic will continue apace. It will need to have effective provisions for Gaelic-medium education or Gaelic in education *otherwise*, as present measures cannot hope to provide the necessary support outwith the family for feasible Gaelic language reproduction. To be effective the ensuing act needs to enable Gaelic to become visible and audible in the social environment of its speakers – in ways which are appropriate nationally and locally, since two-thirds of all Gaelic speakers live outwith the 'heartlands'.

Today the Gaelic language-group faces a crisis. As with many other societies and language-groups today, it is influenced by powerful economic and social forces in the wider world: anglicisation and globalisation. Economic restructuring, trade, commerce, manufacturing, higher education, and world media are promoted via the English-language world-wide. This represents a massive investment not only in technology but in the English language. This is financed by the world domestic product, and assisted by massive and often hidden national and international subsidies of public money. In all this it must be remembered that the Gaelic language-group with a lower total of almost 60,000 and an upper total of just under 100,000 persons is a social entity of distinctive culture which rightly claims provisions in terms of its own cultural infrastructure: education, media, arts and entertainment industries in its own terms – as successors to the ceilidh house, and the *aos-dana*, the learned and bardic orders of former centuries. The means of administration and the civil rights of language-use are just as valid as those for larger speech-communities and language groups. The rights to work, economic sustenance, way-of-life and the pursuit of their own version of happiness are as valid for small language-groups as they are for larger. The Gaelic language-group produces economic wealth and generates an endogenous economic product. It members pay national and local taxes, VAT, excise duty and all the rest. It has the right for its own domestic product and taxation revenue to be used for the support of its own cultural infrastructure and administration of its own way-of-life. In an open and democratic society these realities need to be fully recognised and met.

The challenge for the Gaelic language-group and its institutions now is to recognise the realities of anglicisation and globalisation, but to find ways of effectively working within them and using the logic of the situation to get them to work for Gaelic and to secure a place for itself within them.

Sources
GROS Census Reports 1891-1991, R/SAS Table 40,
GROS Census 2001, Tables: UV12, S206, T27; ONS / NAW 1.3;
ONS England and Wales Census 2001, Tables S133, S137, S139, T15, T29;
E.U. Euromosaic Project 1994/5 (Research Centre Wales, Bangor).

Figure 1: Gaelic Speakers 1881-1991 – numbers by areas of different local incidence of Gaelic speakers

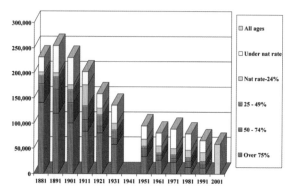

Figure 2: Gaelic speakers by age 1921 – 2001

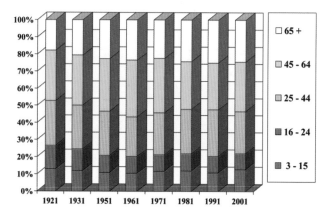

Figure 3: Map – Scotland 2001 Census: Gaelic speakers intercensal change

Figure 4: Gaelic speakers in 2001 Census: areas of residence
Source: GROS Census Scotland 2001 Table UV12

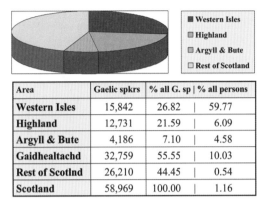

Area	Gaelic spkrs	% all G. sp	% all persons
Western Isles	15,842	26.82	59.77
Highland	12,731	21.59	6.09
Argyll & Bute	4,186	7.10	4.58
Gaidhealtachd	32,759	55.55	10.03
Rest of Scotlnd	26,210	44.45	0.54
Scotland	58,969	100.00	1.16

Figure 5: Gaelic speakers by age: comparison of numbers in 1991 and 2001

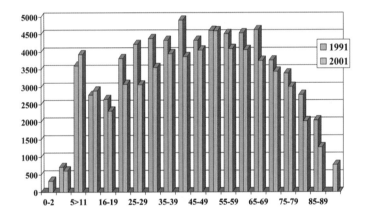

Figure 6: Persons with Gaelic language abilities as % of total age-group in 2001 Census

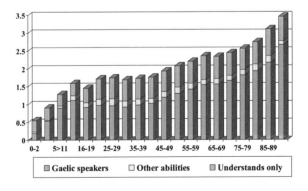

Figure 7: Gaelic language abilities: Scotland 2001

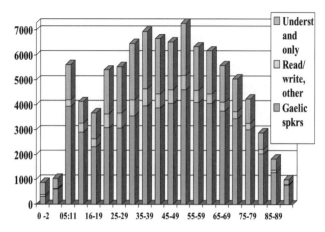

Figure 8: Comparison of Gaelic speakers in 5-15 and 20-44 age-groups: Intergenerational gain / intergenerational ratio

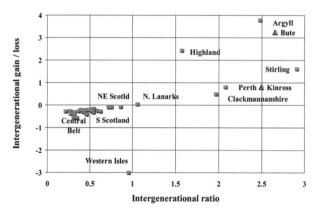

Figure 9: Welsh speakers by age-group: 1971-81-91-2001 Censuses

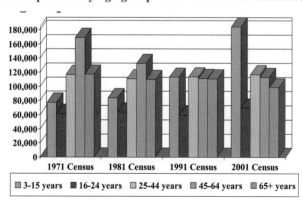

Figure 10: Gaelic speakers by age-group: 1971-81-91-2001 Censuses

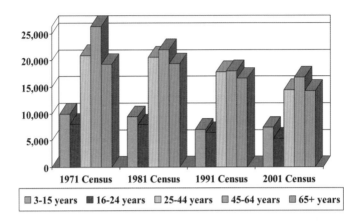

Figure 11: Comparison of Welsh speakers in 3-15 and 16-44 age-groups: Intergenerational gain / intergenerational ratio

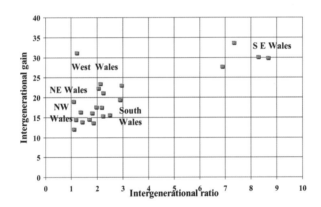

Figure 12: Welsh - intergenerational gain 2001

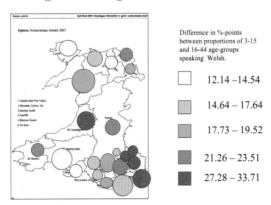

Figure 13: Welsh - intergenerational ratio 2001

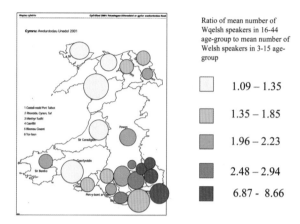

Ratio of mean number of Wqelsh speakers in 16-44 age-group to mean number of Welsh speakers in 3-15 age-group

1.09 – 1.35

1.35 – 1.85

1.96 – 2.23

2.48 – 2.94

6.87 - 8.66

Figure 14: Families with Welsh-speaking children

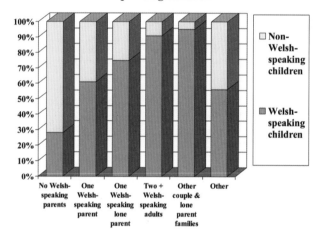

Fig 15: Language in family: Western Isles 1994/5

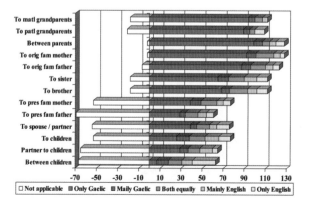

Fig 16: Language in family: Rest of Scotland 1994/55

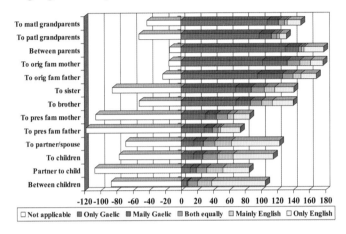

Fig 17: Scotland 2001: Gaelic speakers intergenerational gain/loss

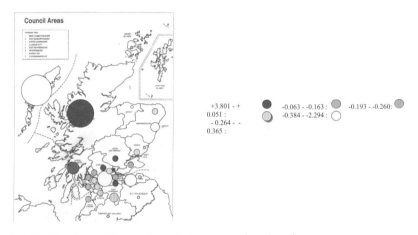

Fig 18: Scotland: Gaelic speakers intergenerational ratio

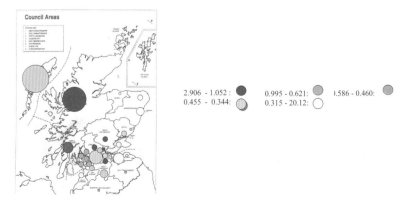

The Celtic Cognates Database

Caoimhín Ó Donnaíle

Summary

A new facility is described which is under development but is already freely available for use on the Sabhal Mòr Ostaig website. The Celtic Cognates Database enables the retrieval of related words across both modern and ancient Celtic languages. It can be used to:
- generate bilingual lists of cognate words which will help learners to learn and retain new vocabulary;
- open up the online dictionary resources of one Celtic language to speakers of another;
- help research the etymology of words.
The Database is currently in the form of a single rectangular table, but other more advanced structures are considered as possibilities for the future.

Introduction

The database is currently available at the address: at http://www.smo.uhi.ac.uk/gaidhlig/faclair/scc/ on the Sabhal Mòr Ostaig website, or it can be found by searching for "Celtic Cognates Database" in the Sabhal Mòr Ostaig site-search.

Here are a few example rows and columns illustrating the format of the database:

Gàidhlig	Gaeilge	Gaelg	Cymraeg	English	Scots
capall	*capall*	*cabbyl*	*ceffyl*	*cavalry*	
ceud	*céad*	*keead*			
fàs	*fás*	*aase*		*wax*	
fear	*fear*	*fer*	*gwir*	*virile*	
gobhal	*gabhal*	*goal*		*gable*	*golach*

(We use the native names Gàidhlig, Gaeilge, Gaelg, Cymraeg, Kernewek, Brezhoneg for Scottish Gaelic, Irish Gaelic, Manx Gaelic, Welsh, Cornish and Breton, respectively.)

A few points:

- There is much work still to be done filling in blanks and finding new cognates.

- The thrust of the work so far has been towards the Celtic languages, but cognates in English, Scots, Latin, German, etc, have been recorded where these have cropped up and this side of things could be greatly expanded.

- For nearly all the languages, it is possible to click on a word in the search results and jump straight to an online dictionary search for the word. Indeed, the desire to unite online dictionaries and other resources in the different Celtic languages has been one of the main motivations for the Celtic Cognates Database. There are still no online dictionaries for Scots or Cornish, but this is about to change for Scots.

Potential uses

Here are just a few examples of potential uses of the Celtic Cognates Database:

- An Irish Gaelic speaker wants to know about the etymology of the Irish word *fuinneog*, but the only Irish Gaelic etymological dictionary in existence, the *Lexique Étymologique de l'Irlandais Ancien*, is written in French, has Old Irish rather than Modern Irish headwords, is not online, and anyway is still missing all words beginning with letters between E and L. MacBain's Scottish Gaelic etymological dictionary is on the Internet and gives the required information under the equivalent Scottish Gaelic word, *uinneag*. The Gaelic cognates database will direct the Irish Gaelic speaker to this information in two clicks.

- A Scottish Gaelic speaker is using Ciarán Ó Duibhín's *Tobar na Gaedhilge* to search for examples of the use of the word *fairge*, but the Tobar na Gaedhilge corpus contains only two works in Scottish Gaelic, so the user wishes to extend the search to works in Irish Gaelic. The Gaelic cognates database will tell him that the corresponding Irish Gaelic word to look for is *farraige*.

- A teacher from Lewis goes to a new job in a Gaelic-medium school in Islay and hears the children using a word as if it had a masculine gender instead of the feminine gender which she would have used herself and which is given in the dictionaries. Are the children making a mistake? With the Gaelic cognates database she can quickly check whether the corresponding Irish Gaelic word is masculine. If it is, what she is hearing is probably a dialect difference rather than a mistake.

- An Irish Gaelic speaker is trying to understand the meaning of a strange-sounding old proverb. There is a fair chance that an equivalent proverb exists in Scottish Gaelic and books of Scottish Gaelic proverbs might give more insight and explanation. The Celtic Cognates Database will help him search.

- A researcher is trying to find out something about the origin of a word in Old Irish, but the pronunciation it might have had is not clear from the spelling in the old manuscripts. The Gaelic cognates database will lead him to the pronunciation of the reflexes in modern Irish, Scottish and Manx Gaelic dialects, which will give him additional information from which to make deductions.

Online resources to which the Cognates database can link

The following are illustrative of some of the Goidelic language dictionaries and other resources which are already online and searchable, and which the Celtic Cognates Database makes accessible to speakers of other Celtic languages.

IRISH GAELIC

An Foclóir Beag
13,000 headword, modern, authoritative Gaelic-Gaelic dictionary. Automatic generation of full declension and conjugation tables.

Focal an Lae
365 common Gaelic words with examples of usage and information on etymology.

SCOTTISH GAELIC

Stòr-dàta Briathrachais Gàidhlig
A terminology database with 100,000 records, although it contains many everyday words as well as technical terminology.

Am Briathrachan Beag
School Gaelic Dictionary by Malcolm MacFarlane, 1912.
A good small general-purpose Gaelic-English dictionary with good grammatical information. 5500 headwords.

MacBain's Gaelic Dictionary
Not a general-purpose dictionary but rather an etymological dictionary with about 15,000 headwords.

Faclair na Pàrlamaid
An English-Gaelic and Gaelic-English dictionary with about 5500 headwords each way. Words useful in government and administration, but also many of general use.

Faclair nan Gnàthasan Cainnte
A searchable Gaelic-English database of over 5000 idioms, phrases and proverbs.

MANX GAELIC

Manx-English dictionary
A 150,000 word Manx-English dictionary — the biggest Gaelic dictionary on the internet.

OLD IRISH

In Dúil Bélrai
An English – Old Irish glossary containing 7700 distinct Old Irish words and a total of 14,500 records.

Technical information

The Celtic Cognates Database is currently held in a mySQL database on a Linux server. PHP is used to provide the link between HTML search forms on WWW and the database itself.

Linking to remote online dictionaries is very straightforward when the remote dictionary search uses the HTTP "GET" method — i.e. URIs containing a question mark, such as:

http://www.smo.uhi.ac.uk/gaidhlig/faclair/bb/lorg.php?facal=kit&seorsa=Beurla

When on the other hand the remote dictionary search uses the HTTP "POST" method, things are not so simple since the search parameters are not now part of the link address. However, this problem can be got round by using a PHP routine which generates a POST request with appropriate parameters.

Current contents

The Celtic Cognates Database currently contains roughly one to two thousand distinct words in each of the Celtic languages (including both forms of Cornish: *Kernewek Kemmyn* and *Kernowek Ûnys*). It is hoped to increase this considerably in the near future for the Goidelic languages. It is particularly easy to generate Scottish Gaelic - Irish Gaelic cognates automatically from dictionaries since the languages are so close and the spelling systems so similar, although the pairs generated need checking by hand. The Database also currently has two to three hundred cognate words from each of: English, German and Latin, plus a handful of Scots cognates. The latter would be particularly worth developing further to record loanwords in each direction. A great deal of work remains to be done in merging records, so that instead of:

Gàidhlig	Gaeilge	Gaelg	Cymraeg	Kernewek
abhainn	*abhainn*	*awin*		
abhainn			*afon*	*avon*
ainm	*ainm*	*ennym*		
ainm	*ainm*		*enw*	*hanow*

for example, we have:

Gàidhlig	Gaeilge	Gaelg	Cymraeg	Kernewek
abhainn	*abhainn*	*awin*	*afon*	*avon*
ainm	*ainm*	*ennym*	*enw*	*hanow*

Some automated procedures need to be developed to help with this.

Other possible formats for the future

A current dilemma

Should we always try to choose words which are most similar, even though they may not be common in the sister language? E.g.:

Gaelg	Gàidhlig	Gaeilge
casley	cosmhail	cosúil
caslys	cosmhaileas	cosúlas

Or should we rather only allow into the database words which are sufficiently common, even though they may not be so closely related?

Gaelg	Gàidhlig	Gaeilge
casley	*coltadh*	*cosúil*
caslys	*coltas*	*cosúlacht*

Solution no. 1 - Groups of words

First construct groups of words in each language, and then link the *wordgroups*, not individual words. E.g.:

Gaelg	Gàidhlig	Gaeilge
casley *caslys*	*cosalachd* *cosamhlachadh* *cosamhlachd* *cosamhlaich*	*cosúil* *cosúlacht* *cosúlaigh*

However, words do not always fall neatly into particular groups. Sometimes they belong partly to two or three different groups. E.g. *caslys-çheerey (*M), *comh-samhlaich (A)*. (For brevity we write (M) to denote Manx Gaelic, (A) to denote Scottish Gaelic, and (E) to denote Irish Gaelic.)

Even apart from pathogenic cases such as these, there is the general question of how wide or narrow the word groups should be made, and there is no simple answer to this.

If the Celtic Cognates Database were to be used as a "translation" aid — and particularly in the case of translation between "Gaedhilg" and "Gaeilge", i.e. between the "full" Classical Modern Irish spelling and the post-1950's abbreviated spelling of the "Caighdeán" official standard — then word groups would not be a good thing at all. What we would need then would be one-to-one equivalents.

Solution no. 2 - Metrics

Here what we do is to acknowledge that things are messy and fuzzy. We just throw every kind of link, be it etymological or morphological, into the database, e.g. *cosley* (M)-*coslys* (M); *cosley* (M)-*cosúil* (E); *cosley* (M)-*coltach* (A). But we give a metric to each pair of words, representing the distance between them. There is a bigger distance between *cosley* (M) and *coltach* (A), for example, than between *cosley* (M) and *cosúil* (E). If we say that the *caslys* (M)-*cosley* (M) distance is 0.2 and that the air *cosley* (M)-*cosúil* (E) distance is 0.5, then the distance between *coslys* (M) and *cosúil* (E) would be 0.7 — unless a shorter route could be found between them. When the database receives a request for all words related to *caslys* (M), it will return all words which are within a certain cut-off distance from *caslys* (M). The words *cosamhlachd* (A) and *coltas* (A) might be within this cut- off distance, whereas *comhsamhlaich* (A) might be too far away to appear in the results.

It would be important to assign metric distances skilfully. Otherwise the words *eadar* (A) and *mogal* (A), for example, might get linked via *Eddyr-Voggyl* (M).

Solution no. 3 - Cognate morphemes

Each language would have its own lexical database, which amongst other things would break each word down into morphemes. The Celtic Cognates Database would record the links between cognate *morphemes*, rather than between cognate words. This third solution is probably the best solution in the long run, although it requires a more sophisticated search system than the present one, and of course requires the work to be done in advance in producing a lexical database for each language with morphemic information.

Other issues for the future

Should etymological laws be included?

Should the database attempt to record "etymological laws" (laws such as Grimm's Law or the Great English Vowel Shift)? — e.g. the steps which an Old Irish word took on its way from Indo-European, or the steps which a Gàidhlig word took on its way from Old Irish? If so, how should we do this?

Lists for learners

What we want for learners are pairs of words which resemble one another, as an aid to learning a second or third Celtic language. However, the Celtic Cognates Database must also record words which are cognate but which do not now resemble each other, so that it can act as a key to dictionaries in a sister language. Therefore, to produce cognates lists for learners it will be necessary to filter out by hand the pairs of words which do not resemble one another.

"New" words

Consider the table:

Gaelg	meaning	Gàidhlig?	Gaeilge?
neu-chiart	*'incorrect'*	*neo-cheart*	*neamh-cheart*
neuchooie	*'unsuitable'*	*neo-iomchaidh*	*neamhiomchuí*
neu-far-skeealaght	*'non-fiction'*		
neu-feeu	*'worthless'*	*neo-fiù*	*neamhfhiú*
neugheyr	*'cheap'*	*neo-dhaor*	*neamhdhaor*
neu-haitnyssagh	*'unpleasant'*	*neo-thaitneach*	*neamhthaitneamhach*
neu-nhee	*'nothing', 'nought', 'zero'*	*neoni*	*neamhní*

In the "Gaelg" column we see genuine commonplace Manx words, but in the "Gàidhlig?" and "Gaeilge?" columns many of the words are "new" words which have been produced from rules which are "semi-productive". They would be readily understood by speakers of Scottish or Irish Gaelic, but they may not feature in any dictionary. We could create thousands of such words. Should we (a) go on like this on the grounds that such words add richness to language and that they provide an explanation of Manx words for Scottish and Irish Gaelic speakers? Or should we (b) leave them out to avoid confusion? Or should we (c) — a compromise option — put them in, but make sure that their "frequency" is recorded as zero or near zero?

Acknowledgements

Work on the Celtic Cognates Database has been assisted by an initial grant of £1000 from Iomairt Cholm Cille (www.colmcille.net). The bulk of the current contents, particularly in the Brythonic languages, have been provided by work by Dilys Powell when she was a student at Sabhal Mòr Ostaig.

How the Montgomeries Lost the Scots Language

Michael Montgomery

In the long century following the introduction of the English Bible to Scottish pulpits in 1560, we know WHAT happened to the Scots language.[1] Much scholarship has shown that inexorably with the advance of English it eroded as the medium of high literature, officialdom, and polite discourse. The complex of distinct Scots orthographic, morphological, and other forms that had become conventionalised in the fifteenth century gradually disappeared. The extinction of this written standard occurred over the course of somewhat more than a century in Scotland (Aitken 1979: 87ff.), but in a generation and a half in Ulster (Montgomery 1992).

In both places spoken Scots went underground, to resurface in writing from time to time as a self-conscious medium to represent speech, first in the early 1700s even as the last vestiges of conventions such as the spelling of *wh-* as *quh-* faded away. This revivalist Scots did not hark back to earlier formal patterns so much as it did to a more colloquial Scots found in popular heroic and comic verse (Aitken 1985: xi). We know little about spoken Scots, except quite indirectly, from the seventeenth to the nineteenth century, but linguistic study suggests that it remained vigorous on the ground in both Scotland and Ulster. Statements that Scots 'converged' with English in the Early Modern Period apply overwhelmingly to writing and cannot be taken as pertaining to speech.

So we know THAT the Scots language was lost in writing, and much about WHEN and WHERE this happened. We also know a good deal about HOW it took place, linguistically speaking, thanks in large part to the work of Devitt (1989). Taking as her time frame the years 1520 to 1659, she investigates across seven 20-year periods the rate and order in which five Scots features (more on these below) declined for five different types of documents, in the following order: religious treatises, official correspondence, private records, private correspondence, and public records (Devitt 1989: 55-58).

Though a truism, it is worth stating that scholars in Scotland (e.g. Aitken) have usually called the general process of attrition 'Anglicisation' (adopted here), while those elsewhere term it 'standardisation'. The one book-length treatment (Devitt 1989) uses the terms to convey different perspectives on the same process, i.e. the replacement of what she calls 'Scots-English' by 'Anglo-English' in Scottish writing and the gradual conformity to English. For Meurman-Solin (1997: 3-4), 'standardisation' occurred in Scotland in the fifteenth century, when in both writing and speech Scots 'de-Anglicised' (i.e. became differentiated from the language of Northern England with Scotland's increasing political and socio-cultural independence), then for writing it 'Anglicised' or converged with English subsequently. For the purposes of her analysis, Devitt must assume that Scots (her 'Scots-English') had already standardised. The Anglicisation process, the first glimmerings of which began somewhat earlier than Devitt's initial tracking point,

---

[1]The author is indebted to Iseabail MacLeod and Bruce Lenman for advice and help with research in Scotland.

involved a wide range of grammatical, phonological, and orthographic characteristics for which only a glance once sufficed to indicate that a document had Scottish rather than English provenance. Scholars of Anglicisation have most often sought to detail the spelling of grammatical features. Many shifts in orthography had no connection to pronunciation (e.g. *ȝ* ==> *y*), others an uncertain correspondence (e.g. *facis* ==> *faces*) or at least an uncertain time lag. Spelling in Scots had begun to fossilise in the early fifteenth century, if not before, in a process that brought not homogeneity, but steady movement toward uniformity, to all aspects of the written word. Not long thereafter, Anglicisation intervened, producing orderly variation working toward another target.

But if we understand much of the THAT, the WHERE, the WHEN, even the HOW of Anglicisation as it pertained to genres and linguistic features, we know little about its dynamics on the human level. To what extent can we detect variation between writers or groups of writers as they shifted from Scots to English? Thanks to the work of Devitt and Meurman-Solin, the broad chronological and textual dimensions of the process are now understood, but the social ones much less so. To what extent might the correspondence of one extended family mirror Anglicisation as a whole? The title I have chosen is ambiguous. To say that the Montgomeries 'lost' the Scots language raises issues that at the same time are social (an individual's conscious or unconscious choice of models), methodological (how texts can be found and analysed in a meaningful way), and linguistic (the patterns by which Scots forms were supplanted by English ones). Like many aristocratic counterparts, in the seventeenth century the Montgomeries gradually shifted their literacy from Scots to English, so that by the early 1660s only an occasional Scots form dotted their writing. Their surviving letters reveal no overtly expressed reason for abandoning Scots, but the shift can hardly have been brought about by forces differing from those that caught up many other Scottish families, e.g., increased travel to England and the Continent, greater access to English reading materials, increased contacts of all sorts (including marriage) between the upper classes of England and Scotland, and so forth. The Montgomeries present a microcosm of the expanding world of Scottish nobility in the seventeenth century after the Union of the Crowns.

Thus, the most important and intriguing questions about Anglicisation that remain, I believe, involve WHO led the transition from Scots to English forms. Was it, for example, men or women? By examining the shift from Scots to English in the private letters of one family written over the better part of a century, perhaps we can capture a microcosmic view of Anglicisation and answer this question.

The material for our exploration comprises 103 letters written by the Montgomeries and their relations by marriage between 1576 and 1665; of these, 57 were from 17 men and 46 from 13 women. A prominent family of Norman extraction, the Montgomeries came to North Ayrshire in the twelfth century. A branch crossed to east County Down in 1605 and so, like many other families of the Southwest Lowlands, they and their language bridged the Irish Channel. Some were active in the War of the Three Kingdoms. Two lengthy letters of Hugh Montgomerie of the Great Ards detail from Comber the precarious state of affairs following the Irish Rebellion of October 1642. The family's correspondence, which mixes political, domestic, social and other concerns, is centered around Alexander, sixth Earl of Eglinton, and his relatives. His 17 letters span nearly fifty years, from 1612 to 1658. Such a corpus of letters lends itself to many avenues of investigation: for example, how individuals shifted to English during their lifetime (as their reading and social contacts would have widened) or whether the sex of the addressee, the purpose or motivation of the letter, the deferential stance of a writer, or the difference or sameness of generation correlated with a writer's choice of Scots or English. But space limits our consideration to whether, for the Montgomeries, it was men or women in the lead in Anglicisation for three generations of writers.

As already noted, early in the period of our consideration, the Scottishness of any letter of the Montgomerie family was discernible at a glance. Here is one example:

Alexander, first Earl of Linlythgow, to his daughter Anna Countess of Eglintoun, 1st November 1612

Loveing daughter — I receavit zour lettir, together with ane frome my lady zour good mother, quha desires me to meit her ladyship into Edinburgh upone Weddnisday nixtt; quhich I shall nocht omitt, if my health will permit me, as I have wrettin to her ladyship, and give the best assestance lyes in me to the furtherance of zour housbands affaires. Bott within these thre nightis, there is ane dollour falling downe into the right syd of my head, with the pape into my halse, that stayis me from rest, eatting, or drinking. I perceave my lord zour housbond is not certane of his returne; therfor we moun take the greatter care of his turnes at this terme: and albeit they go sumquhat hardlie as zitt quhair he is, there is no dowpt bott it will turne wtherwayes shortlie. I am verie dilligent to have money to zou in tyme, albeit I may nocht travell my self; and sall leave no thing vndone to the furtherance therof. So for the present, my verie loveing dewtie remembred, I committ zou to Gods protectiowne, and resthethe evir,

Your ladyships loving father,

Half a century later, only a few Scots forms could be found in their writing. Thus, the Montgomerie family presents an intriguing case study for tracking Anglicisation.

It is to William Fraser, later knighted, that we are indebted for transcription, organisation, and commentary on letters, charters, and other documents of Montgomerie family importance. His two-volume edition *Memorials of the Montgomeries* (1859) was one of the first of a long and magnificent series of collected private papers from major landed families of Scotland. Since manuscript versions of the letters are held in the private library of the Earl of Eglinton, the originals have not been accessible to the author of this paper. Though they were produced a century and a half ago, both internal and external factors argue for the validity of Fraser's transcriptions for linguistic purposes. Individual letters exhibit extensive variation between Scottish and English forms and occasionally have three or even four variants, so Fraser apparently did not regularise word forms. It might be thought that noble families like the Montgomeries dictated letters to assistants or secretaries and that we can infer nothing about their own language from those selected by Fraser. However, according to Bruce Lenman, Professor of

Modern History at St. Andrew's University and a specialist in seventeenth-century Scotland, the letters were almost certainly written by the signatories. He knows of no household in Early Modern Britain that employed a secretary or scribe. Even the royal letters were often written by the monarch.

Then there is the testimony of Fraser himself on his editorial method that argues for the validity of the transcriptions:

> In printing the Letters and the Charters, the object of the Editor has been to give the text of the original writs as accurately as possible. But many of the Charters and other papers are in Latin, and in accordance with the practice of the period in which they written, the words are frequently contracted. Such words have been printed at full length. In the original documents the punctuation is often defective and erroneous, and the use of capital letters capricious. In printing the punctuation has been corrected, and the modern usage with regard to capital letters has been followed. With these exceptions, no alterations have been made. The spelling, however different in many cases from that now in use, has been preserved throughout, so that the print gives a faithful representation of the original documents. (Fraser 1859: viii)

Confining a study to variation within a single genre between members of a single family controls for social class and other variables and enables us to isolate some social dimensions of Anglicisation. Because only private correspondence had more than a small handful of female authors (in the case at hand, we have a roughly equal and sizable number of documents and authors from each sex), it represents the only type of text for which we may hope to compare the behavior of men and women and discover who was more conservative and who was leading language change. The intersection of gender variation and Anglicisation in the period is not an altogether new question. In an early study using her *Helsinki Corpus of Older Scots*, Meurman-Solin (1993: 18) concluded that 'women seem to be more conservative in their spelling practices in the period of intense anglicisation in the Scots language, namely in the subperiod 1570-1640', but later, in a preliminary study (2001) using her *Corpus of Early Scottish Women's Writings*, she backed away from this position, stating that the written Scots of both men and women was too heterogeneous to be compared meaningfully. One cannot deny the value of considering individual variation, but the present study, with its greater exercise of control, may be expected to reveal greater homogeneity among men and women than did Meurman-Solin's material. The choice of private correspondence has at least two other major advantages over public correspondence or other genres. Not only did it apparently not rely on copyists or secretaries, it was not subject to the normative editing of contemporary publishers. Moreover, as the genre that Devitt found to be next to public records in lateness to Anglicise, private correspondence should offer a richer vein of Scots forms. As a result, we may be able to achieve a more sensitive and detailed understanding of the process.

Even with comparatively rich data and with controls over the genre and the social profile of the authors, the question of who led the shift to English faces obstacles and complexities, as there is much we don't know about the period.

Among these are the following: other than the English Bible, what exactly were people reading or hearing? what was the role of written models? what was the influence of teachers or tutors?

Tracking Anglicisation

Any variable used to track Anglicisation should meet three criteria: a distinct Scots variant (or cluster of closely related variants), a distinct English target variant, and a reasonable number of contexts in which the variable occurs. Among some of the possible variants to examine are the following:

Form of past-tense copula/auxiliary *be* (Scots *wes/war* vs. English *was/were*)

Demonstrative pronouns (Scots t*hir/thae* vs. English *these/those*)
    <sh> (Scots *sche* vs. English *she*)
    /x/ (Scots *micht* vs. English *might*)
    <y> (Scots *ʒour* vs. English *your*)

Presumably because of the frequency of their contexts, Devitt chose not these, but five other variables. These are listed below, with examples of the Scots forms from the Montgomery letters, if these occur.

Present participle: Scots *-and* vs. English *-ing*: the Montgomerie letters have no forms in *-and* [2].

Negative markers: Scots *nocht* vs. English *not* and Scots *na/nae* vs. English *no*:

I perceave my lord zour housband is *nocht* certane of his return. (Alexander, first Earl of Linlithgow, to his daughter Anna, Countess of Eglintoun, 1st November 1612 [3])

I heir be my lord that it is lyk to tak *na* effect. (Eleanor, Countess of Linlithgow, to Anna, Countess of Eglintoun, her daughter, 24th November 1612)

Indefinite article preceding consonants: Scots *ane* vs. English *a*: [4]

I wish Her Maiestie may be *ane* good agent for you. (Anna, Countess of Eglintoune to Alexander, sixth Earl, her husband, 11th November 1612)

Preterites and past participles of weak verbs: Scots *-it/-itt/-yt* vs. English *-ed*:

---

[2] A few instances of forms in -in were discounted as ambiguous.
[3] The descriptive details of each letter are taken verbatim from Fraser's volume.
[4] Because the numeral has the same form in Scots, it is sometimes difficult to distinguish article *ane* from numeral *ane*. For the purpose of this study, all questionable cases are ignored. In her study, Devitt did not distinguish whether article *ane* preceded a consonant or a vowel; in other words, she considered the English equivalents to be either *a* or *an*.

I *reseuit* zowris the fourt of this instant, wnderstanding therby my lord my
sone, zour self, and all the bairnes to be in guid helth, quhairof I wes very
glaid. (Margaret Countess Dowager of Wintoun to Anna Countess of
Eglintoun, her daughter-in-law, 5th March 1615)

I feir that thir dolorous dayes hes *hinderit* zow that zour turnes ar not done.
(Margaret, Lady Seutone, Countess Dowager of Wintoun, to Alexander, sixth
Earl of Eglintoun, her son, nineteenth November 1612)

Spelling of relative clause markers and related forms: Scots *quh-* vs. English
wh-:

albeit they go *sumquhat* hardlie as *zitt quhair* he is, thair is no doupt that butt
it will turne wthirwayes shortlie. (Alexander, first Earl of Linlithgow, to his
daughter Anna, Countess of Eglintoun, 1st November 1612)

Any number of other variables are potential choices for investigation. In order
to provide comparability with Devitt's work, four of her variables will be analysed
here, along with four others: noun plurals, and three others closely related ones
that involve two constraints affecting present-tense verbal concord: lexical verbs
(including *have*) having third-plural subjects, copula/auxiliary *be* having third-
plural subjects, and verbs whose subject is a pronoun in another clause or implied.[5]
The system underlying these concord patterns, which has prevailed historically in
northern England, Scotland, and parts of Ireland, is sometimes known as the
'northern present-tense rule'. To put in simplest terms, this rule marks concord
when the verb has a third-plural subject other than *they* (as *Soldiers goes* vs. *they
go*) or when the verb is separated from its subject, especially by a clause (*as they
come and goes*). This system governs concord by the person, number, type, and
proximity of the subject, unlike its counterpart in English. (For a historical
account, see Montgomery 1994.)

Noun plural suffixes: Scots *-is* vs. English *-s/-es*:

Resave twa *lettris* frome zour Ladyships brother, Sir James ... (Alexander,
first Earl of Linlythgow, to Anna Countess of Eglintoun, his daughter, 28th
May 1620)

Present-tense concord with third-person-plural noun subjects for lexical verbs
and *have*: Scots *-s/hes* vs. English *have*.[6]

all matires *gos* very weill in Jermany ... (Hugh Lord Montgomerie to
Alexander, sixth Earl of Elgintoun, his father, 6th April 1633)

Your manay caynd favouris *hes* med me afttin weich that I micht heue the
occation to geiue your lordship testimonie of my wilingnes to repay it hom.

---

[5] Many, but by no means all, of these implied subjects occurred in the complimentary close
of letters.
[6] In the letters five forms end in *-th* (e.g. *they doeth, horsemen doth*).

(Lady Anna Cunynghame, Marchioness of Hamilton, to Alexander, sixth Earl of Eglintoun, 1634)

Present-tense concord with copula/auxiliary *be* with third-person-plural subjects: Scots *is* vs. English *are*.

his longe trubils *is* nov vorin neir a end. (Lady Isabella Setoune, Countess of Perth, to Anna Countess of Eglintoun, 9th December 1617)

Because the number of present-tense verbs with non-adjacent or implied pronoun subjects is fairly small, all verb types are combined for this variable. Thus, we find Scots *-is/hes/is* vs. English *i/have/are*.

Nocht farder, but remember my comendationis to my Lady Seutone, zour gud mother, and me Lady Perthe: *cmmittis* zow to God, and *restis* zour evir assurit lovinge mother ... (Eleanor, Countess of Linlithgow, to Anna, Countess of Eglintoun, her daughter, 24th November 1612)

I haue acquentted his lordship thairwith at lenthe; and *hes* schawin his lordship that double quhiche zour Lordship sent to me ... (George, third Earl of Wintoun, to Alexander, sixth Earl of Eglintoun, his brother, seventeenth August 1626)

I recevet yovr ladyships letter of the fvyeth of Aryle, and *is glad* to heir of your ladyships vilfair. (James Leuingstoune to Anna Countess of Eglintoune, his sister, 4 May 1616)

Before turning to the analysis, it is necessary to identify four caveats and limitations, two external and two internal, that arose in the process of classifying and tabulating the data. First, presentation of data from thirty individuals writing across several decades inevitably disperses it rather thinly in some cases, limiting the possibility of generalisation and giving undue weight to effects of individual variation. Second, Fraser tells us the date of composition of each letter, but not the age of writers, from which we might more precisely infer the period of their acquiring literacy. For this reason, data are presented in two sets of tables, by decade (based on the date of the letter) and the generation of the writer.[7] Third, most variables combine unrelated base forms, and shifts from Scots variants to English ones may be finer grained than detectible in the data at hand. For example, Scots forms in *quh-* may not have moved en masse toward *wh-*, but rather in a staggered manner that reflected a progression within this variable; only a much larger corpus of material can throw light on this matter. Or they may be phonologically influenced: for example, *-it* may have lingered longer preceding

---

[7] Using information from Fraser's headnotes and internal evidence, the writers were divided into three generations, which cut across the decades: 1) older writers, consisting of the parents and parents-in-law of Alexander, sixth Earl of Eglinton (1576-1620); 2) Alexander, his wife, and their siblings (1612-1658); and 3) the sons of Alexander (1632-1665) and other younger members of the family.

voiceless consonants than voiced ones. A finer grained division of data within each variable analysis would divide it to a point beyond which meaningful patterns would be much more unlikely to appear. Finally, the seventeenth century was a period of great orthographic flux even beyond that created by competition between Scots and English forms. For this reason alone, we expect to find many variations. Because of the language shift taking place and the instability of spelling in both Scots and English, we find a number of intermediate forms:

-*in* for present participles (discounted, because this ending could represent either Scots or English);

-*et* and -*id* for preterites and past participles of weak verbs (-*et* counted as Scots, -*id* as English);

for relative clause markers, *qu-, qv-,* and *qh-* (counted as Scots)[8] and *vh-, uh-* and *u-* (counted as English);

-*th* for verbal concord (discounted because it is English in form, but sometimes patterns according to the Scots concord rule).

To subsume all these structurally unrelated developments under the single rubric of 'Anglicisation' misses some details, especially in a study of our somewhat limited depth, but the process has many complexities that bear follow-up study of the structural history of specific variables. In some cases we can identify more than one transitional form, e.g. from Scots *quha* to *quho* to English *who*, or Scots *quhilk* to Scots *whilk* to English *which*.

Because Fraser's collection contains only four letters in Scots pre-dating 1612 (one from 1576, one from 1583, and two from 1584), our scrutiny will concentrate on the period 1610 to 1660. The similarities to Devitt's findings both across genres and for private correspondence **(Tables 1-3)** are clear, exhibiting roughly the same progression of decline and rapid change for most variables in the first half of the seventeenth century. The loss of Scots present participle -*and* occurred first, followed by the negative markers *nocht* and *na*, while the indefinite article *ane* remained the strongest at mid-century. **Tables 4-11 and 12-19** display, respectively, data for men and women writers from the Montgomerie letters according to decade of composition (eight decades for men, five for women) and generation (three for each sex). Beyond the utility of the latter presentation in revealing a clearer progression for most variables is its greater validity in classifying writers by their approximate period of acquiring literacy. These sixteen tables present (for every feature other than negative markers) the percentages of Scots variants (the notation '--' indicates no contexts in which the variable occurred).

1) Negative markers. **Table 4** indicates that *nocht* had all but disappeared in the letters, occurring only four times in the 1610s and not thereafter. *Na(e)* was somewhat hardier, especially among men, but the only occurrence after the 1620s was in a 1642 letter by Alexander, the sixth Earl, oldest member of the middle

---

[8] Thus, *quho*, which marks a partial shift toward *who*, is classified as Scots, whereas *whilk*, an intermediate form between *quhilk* and *which*, is considered English

generation. Neither form was used by the younger generation (**Table 12**).

2) Indefinite article. *Ane* was the majority form of the article preceding consonants well into the seventeenth century (**Table 5**). Though based on fewer contexts, the percentages for *ane* are consistently higher for women. **Table 13** shows the form disappearing rapidly across the generations for men, but much less so for women, for whom it was holding its own among younger writers.

3) The Scots suffix *-it* on the preterites and past participles of weak verbs (combined in this analysis[9]) was the dominant form through the 1620s, thereafter declining for both women and men. The rapidity of the loss among the latter is disguised in **Table 6**, because the 22% figure for the 1640s reflects largely the usage of Alexander, sixth Earl, again the most senior member of the middle generation (14 of the 23 examples of *-it* come from him). Here again, aggregating the data by generation (**Table 14**) shows a clearer pattern and, as for indefinite article ane, women retaining the Scots form more steadily.

4) The spelling of relative clause markers and related forms in *quh-* (e.g. *sumquhat, quhither*) is a hallmark feature of Scots that for the Montgomeries was eroding dramatically for both men and women in the 1620s and 1630s (**Table 7**). Its apparent resurgence among women in the 1650s is attributable largely to four letters of Mary Leslie, Lady Montgomerie, wife of Alexander, sixth Earl (she had 28 forms in *quh-* but only five in *wh-*). **Table 15** shows a steady decline across generations for the Scots variant, with men slightly leading the shift to English.

5) **Table 8** indicates that the noun plural suffix *-is* was a minority form for the Montgomeries by the 1610s. Thereafter its replacement by English *-s/-es* was erratic by decade and by generation (**Table 16**). For this variable no apparent pattern for men vs. women emerges.

6) Arguably the most persistent grammatical feature of Scots in the Montgomerie letters is the complex rule for subject-verb concord whereby the suffix *-s/-is* appeared on present-tense verbs except when their subject was an adjacent personal pronoun. According to this rule, *-s/-is* (or by analogy *hes* and *is*) should rarely occur in Scots when a personal pronoun is adjacent to the verb, and this is what the Montgomerie letters show. Since there is only one exception to this rule in 51 possible contexts having an adjacent *they* and never for other pronoun subjects, these figures are not reported in tables. That one exception is as follows:

sua thay *desyrs* not to be knavin (Alexander, first Earl of Linlithgow, to Anna, Countess of Eglintoun, his daughter, 6th December 1619)

Montgomery (1994) finds that this rule occurred as early as the early fifteenth century for lexical verbs and *have* (i.e. producing the form *hes*). It was soon thereafter extended to present-tense copula/auxiliary *be*, but did not reach completion (pp. 89-91). As seen in **Tables 9-10**, a reverse process appeared underway by the seventeenth century, with the Scots pattern eroding for *be* first, quite likely because it was weaker there. Once again, the somewhat disjointed figures for each decade fall into a clearer pattern when broken down by generation (**Tables 17-18**), which show men shifting to English patterns ahead of women.

---

[9] Past participles represent the majority of tokens in the Montgomerie letters. A cursory examination suggests that they do not appear to pattern differently from preterites in the choice of suffix.

Tables 17-19 indicate that regardless of verb type or proximity of the subject to the verb, both men and women maintained the Scots system for concord through the period under consideration. Unfortunately, the lack of family letters in Fraser's collection beyond 1665 prevents us from tracking it further.

For the Montgomeries overall, a comparison of Scots and English forms for eight variables suggests that it is men who by the end of our period approached full Anglicisation first. For only negative forms were they more conservative than women, and then only slightly more so. The movement toward English was by no means a matter of men taking an early lead and maintaining that for subsequent generations, however. For all variables the oldest generation of men and women shows more or less parity, suggesting that their acquisition of literacy, reading habits, and orientation to their audience was quite similar. Except for verbal concord, figures for the middle generation show steady movement toward English by both sexes, but neither appears to be ahead in general. Men were less Scottish for relative clause markers (34% vs. 41% for women), but women more Scottish for indefinite articles (33% vs. 67%). For only verbal concord for both sexes and indefinite articles for men were Scottish forms in the majority for the middle generation.

A completely different picture emerges for the younger generation, wherein men consistently had outpaced women in the march toward English. For indefinite articles, men were only 5% Scottish, women 42%. For weak verb suffixes, men were at 6%, women 24%, and so on. Younger men provide much more data than younger women, a reflection of the fact that the collection contains several long letters from the sons of Alexander, the sixth Earl: in particular Hugh, writing from Germany and Ireland, and James, from Paris. They are largely responsible for the radical disjuncture between middle-generation and younger men writers (from 67% Scottish to only 5% for indefinite articles, 42% to 6% for weak verb endings, etc.) Younger Montgomerie correspondents represented the first generation born in the seventeenth century. They found themselves in a rapidly expanding world and joined it. As a result, their written language and that of their generation in Scotland took an accelerated step toward English and did not look back.

While of necessity the writing of a single extended family represents a very finite body of data, a study of letters by the Montgomeries has much to suggest about the progress of Anglicisation and in itself opens up a valuable way to explore the process, by using transcriptions produced by William Fraser well over a century ago. The Montgomeries were hardly responsible for promoting the decline of written Scots, yet they played their part in one of the major language shifts in Britain in recent centuries.

References

Aitken, A. J. (1979) 'Scottish Speech: A Historical View with Special Reference to the Standard English of Scotland' in A. J. Aitken and Tom McArthur (eds), *Languages of Scotland*, Edinburgh: Chambers, 85-118.

Aitken, A. J. (1985) 'A History of Scots' in Mairi Robinson et al. (eds), *The Concise Scots Dictionary*, Aberdeen: Aberdeen University Press, ix-xvi.

Aitken, A. J. (1997) 'The Pioneers of Anglicised Speech in Scotland: A Second Look'. *Scottish Language* 16: 1-36.

Devitt, Amy (1989) *Standardizing Written English. Diffusion in the Case of Scotland* 1520-1659. Cambridge: Cambridge University Press.

Donaldson, Gordon (1985) *Sir William Fraser: The Man and His Work.* Edinburgh: Edina Press.

Fraser, William (1859) *Memorial of the Montgomeries.* 2 vols. Edinburgh: privately published.

Meurman-Solin, Anneli (1993) *Variation and Change in Early Scots Prose.* Annales Academiae Scientarum Fennicae Dissertationes Humanarum Litterarum 65, Helsinki: Suomalainen Tiedeakatemia.

Meurman-Solin, Anneli (1997) 'Differentiation and standardisation in early Scots'. *The Edinburgh History of the Scots Language*, ed. by Charles Jones, Edinburgh: Edinburgh University Press. 3-23.

Meurman-Solin, Anneli (2001) 'Women as Informants in the Reconstruction of Geographically and Socioculturally Conditioned Language Variation and Change in Sixteenth- and Seventeenth-Century Scots', *Scottish Language* 16: 20-46.

Montgomery, Michael (1992) 'The Anglicisation of Scots in Early Seventeenth Century Ulster'. *Studies in Scottish Literature* 26: 50-64.

Montgomery, Michael (1994) 'The Evolution of Verb Concord in Scots', in Alexander Fenton and Donald A. MacDonald (eds),. *Studies in Scots and Gaelic: Proceedings of the Third International Conference on the Languages of Scotland.* Edinburgh: Canongate Academic, 81-95.

Table 1: Prevalence of Scots forms (Devitt 1989, after Peters 1997:64) (in percentages)

	1600	1659
	%	%
Present Participle	5	1
Negative Marker	43	5
Indefinite Article	60	26
Weak Preterite/Past Participle	77	13
Relative Clause Marker	83	17

Table 2: Prevalence of Scots forms in Personal Correspondence (Devitt 1989:57) (in percentages)

	1600-1619	1640-1659
	%	%
Present Participle	5	0
Negative Marker	30	0
Indefinite Article	68	37
Weak Preterite/Past Participle	90	17
Relative Clause Marker	90	31

Table 3: Prevalence of Scots forms in Montgomerie Letters (in percentages)

	Before 1610	After 1650
	%	%
Present Participle	0	0
Negative Marker	60	0
Indefinite Article	--	12
Weak Preterite/Past Participle	94	3
Relative Clause Marker	100	1
*Noun Plural	10	11
*Verbal Concord with Lexical Verbs/*have*	--	80
*Verbal Concord with *be*	--	67
*Verbal Concord with Pronoun Subjects	100	100

(*not investigated by Devitt)

Table 4: Negative Markers in the Montgomerie Letters

	MEN					WOMEN				
Decade	No. Letter	*nocht*	*not*	*na*	*no*	No. Letter	*nocht*	*not*	*na*	*no*
1570s	0	0	0	0	2					
1580s	1	1	0	2	0					
1610s	9	3	24	4	4	18	1	81	1	15
1620s	2	0	4	1	1	3	0	8	0	5
1630s	5	0	10	0	2	3	0	7	0	0
1640s	12	0	63	1	5	5	0	10	0	3
1650s	7	0	44	0	6	5	0	29	0	3
1660s	2	0	5	0	0					

Table 5: Indefinite Articles Before Consonants in the Montgomerie Letters

	MEN				WOMEN			
Decade	No. Letters	*ane*	*a*	*% ane*	No. Letters	*ane*	*a*	*% ane*
1610s	7	8	3	74	11	22	14	61
1620s	2	4	0	100	1	1	0	100
1630s	3	4	8	33	3	8	0	100
1640s	10	17	63	21	2	4	3	57
1650s	6	8	31	21	4	1	30	3
1660s	2	0	12	0				

Table 6: Weak Verb Preterites / Past Participles in the Montgomerie Letters

	MEN				WOMEN			
Decade	No. Letters	*-it*	*-ed*	*% -it*	No. Letters	*-it*	*-ed*	*% -it*
1570s	1	5	0	100				
1580s	2	12	1	92				
1610s	13	42	17	71	22	71	39	65
1620s	2	9	8	53	3	10	0	100
1630s	8	0	52	0	7	12	18	40
1640s	14	23	83	22	7	5	21	19
1650s	7	0	60	0	6	3	25	11
1660s	3	0	17	0				

Table 7: Spelling of Relative Clause Markers in the Montgomerie Letters

Decade	MEN				WOMEN			
	No. Letters	*quh-*	*wh-*	*% quh-*	No. Letters	*quh-*	*wh-*	*% quh-*
1570s	1	2	0	100				
1580s	2	6	0	100				
1610s	10	33	6	85	18	38	29	57
1620s	2	9	1	90	3	7	19	27
1630s	8	13	29	31	3	2	1	67
1640s	16	13	107	11	6	1	27	4
1650s	8	0	50	0	5	34	10	77
1660s	3	0	19	0				

Table 8: Noun Plural Suffixes in the Montgomerie Letters

Decade	MEN				WOMEN			
	No. Letters	*-is*	*-s/-es*	*% -is*	No. Letters	*-is*	*-s/-es*	*% -is*
1570s	1	2	0	100				
1580s	2	15	0	100				
1610s	14	25	67	27	20	26	69	28
1620s	2	9	12	43	2	2	2	50
1630s	10	1	59	2	6	11	11	50
1640s	16	21	160	12	7	0	21	0
1650s	6	7	75	8	6	7	45	13
1660s	2	2	26	7				

Table 9: Present-Tense Verbal Concord with Third-Person-Plural Noun Subjects in the Montgomerie Letters (lexical verbs and *have*)

Decade	MEN				WOMEN			
	No. Letters	*-s*	$\emptyset$	*% -s*	No. Letters	*-s*	$\emptyset$	*% -s*
1570s	0	0	0	--				
1580s	0	0	0	--				
1610s	4	5	0	100	9	13	1	93
1620s	1	0	1	0	1	1	0	100
1630s	7	7	0	100	3	8	0	100
1640s	8	11	11	50	2	6	0	100
1650s	3	3	1	75	3	6	1	86
1660s	0	0	0	--				

Table 10: Present-Tense Verbal Concord with Third-Person-Plural Noun Subjects in the Montgomerie Letters (copula/auxiliary *be***)**

	MEN				WOMEN			
Decade	No. Letters	*is*	*are*	*% is*	No. Letters	*is*	*are*	*% is*
1570s	0	0	0	--				
1580s	0	0	0	--				
1610s	7	4	5	44	13	7	13	35
1620s	1	0	1	0	2	1	4	20
1630s	11	4	12	25	3	3	3	50
1640s	12	3	33	8	5	4	2	67
1650s	6	10	2	83	2	2	2	50
1660s	1	0	2	0				

Table 11: Present-Tense Verbal Concord with Non-Adjacent/Implied Pronoun Subjects in the Montgomerie Letters (lexical verbs, *have***, and copula/auxiliary** *be***)**

	MEN				WOMEN			
Decade	No. Letters	*-s/is*	∅	*% -s/is*	No. Letters	*-s/is*	∅	*% -s/is*
1570s	1	1	0	100				
1580s	1	1	0	100				
1610s	5	12	2	86	9	21	0	100
1620s	2	5	0	100	3	2	1	67
1630s	10	11	3	79	7	11	0	100
1640s	7	3	6	33	2	2	0	100
1650s	0	0	0	--	2	2	0	100
1660s	0	0	0	--				

Table 12: Negative Markers by Generation

	MEN					WOMEN				
Generation	No. Letters	*nocht*	*not*	*na*	*no*	No. Letters	*nocht*	*not*	*na*	*no*
older	3	4	3	1	1	7	0	28	1	12
middle	17	0	65	7	8	15	1	78	0	8
younger	20	0	82	0	11	12	0	29	0	6

Table 13: Indefinite Articles Before Consonants by Generation

Generation	MEN				WOMEN			
	No. Letters	*ane*	*a*	*% ane*	No. Letters	*ane*	*a*	*% ane*
older	2	2	0	100	6	11	1	92
middle	18	34	17	67	7	17	35	33
younger	10	5	100	5	8	8	11	42

Table 14: Weak Verb Preterites / Past Participles by Generation

Generation	MEN				WOMEN			
	No. Letters	*-it*	*-ed*	*% -it*	No. Letters	*-it*	*-ed*	*% -it*
older	6	23	3	88	10	55	2	96
middle	24	59	86	42	17	28	45	38
younger	20	9	150	6	18	18	56	24

Table 15: Spelling of Relative Clause Markers by Generation

Generation	MEN				WOMEN			
	No. Letters	*quh-*	*wh-*	*% quh-*	No. Letters	*quh-*	*wh-*	*% quh-*
older	6	18	0	100	9	36	1	97
middle	22	36	70	34	12	37	54	41
younger	22	22	142	13	14	9	33	21

Table 16: Noun Plural Suffixes by Generation

Generation	MEN				WOMEN			
	No. Letters	*-is*	*-s/-es*	*% -s*	No. Letters	*-is*	*-s/-es*	*% -is*
older	6	25	4	86	9	21	39	35
middle	27	52	176	23	15	10	61	14
younger	20	5	219	2	18	15	69	18

Table 17: Present-Tense Verbal Concord with Third-Person-Plural Noun Subjects (lexical verbs and *have*)

Generation	MEN				WOMEN			
	No. Letters	-*s*	∅	% -*s*	No. Letters	-*s*	∅	% -*s*
older	1	1	0	100	9	18	1	95
middle	9	10	1	91	5	8	1	89
younger	13	14	12	54	4	8	0	100

Table 18: Present-Tense Verbal Concord with Third-Person-Plural Noun Subjects (copula/auxiliary *be*)

Generation	MEN				WOMEN			
	No. Letters	*is*	*are*	% *is*	No. Letters	*is*	*are*	% *is*
older	0	0	0	--	9	5	8	38
middle	23	11	18	38	7	6	4	60
younger	15	9	32	22	9	6	4	60

Table 19: Present-Tense Verbal Concord with Non-Adjacent/Implied Pronoun Subjects (lexical verbs, *have*, and copula/auxiliary *be*)

Generation	MEN				WOMEN			
	No. Letters	-*s/is*	∅	% -*s/is*	No. Letters	-*s/is*	∅	% -*s/is*
older	5	9	0	100	11	14	0	100
middle	14	16	4	80	9	11	1	92
younger	7	3	4	43	3	4	0	100

Demonstrative Use and Variation in the Lower Garioch

Sandra McRae

1. Introduction

Traditionally in Northern Scots no distinction is made between the singular and plural demonstrative forms. Therefore we have a situation where *this* and *that* are used when referring to both singular and plural entities, as opposed to standard English *these* and *those*, or Central Scots *thir* and *thae*. It is interesting to note that plural *this* and *that* may occur both when native speakers use their local dialect and when they are speaking what is otherwise Scottish Standard English (SSE) with few dialectal elements. The following examples illustrate two different speech contexts in which local demonstrative forms may occur. If you contrast sentences (i) and (ii) you will find that (i) is predominantly Aberdeenshire Scots:

(i). Fit hiv ye deen tae *iss briks*?

whilst (ii) is mostly SSE:

(ii). What have ye done tae *this trousers*?

but both use the local proximal form *this (iss)*. Sentences (iii) and (iv) show the same contrast but with the local distal form in both cases:

(iii). *Aat hooses* is bein caaed doon the morn.
(iv). *That houses* are bein knocked down tomorrow.

Today, the linguistic situation in Aberdeenshire is more diverse. The local forms are very often used alongside the standard forms *these* and *those* with the addition of non-standard *them* being used as a distal pronoun and determiner. Furthermore, many native speakers still use the distal form *thon* or *yon* when referring to objects or concepts which are further away.

My research is centred in and around the Burgh of Inverurie in the Lower Garioch (sixteen miles north-west of Aberdeen) where I have been examining the demonstrative use of a cross section of the speech community. Traditionally described as a rural market town, Inverurie has expanded rapidly in the last twenty years to cope with the large influx of migrants arriving in the area on account of the oil industry and related employment opportunities. Nonetheless, whilst on one hand providing a commuter base for those employed in and around the City of Aberdeen, Inverurie has continued to retain the sense of a small town community to a certain extent, prospering from local agriculture and light industry.

Summary of objectives

This paper will summarise the methods used in gathering my linguistic data, before examining the binary relationship between the local and standard demonstrative forms within the speech community. Here, particular attention will be paid to the contrasting roles played by these forms in relation to age-group. Furthermore, it will look at the way in which individual speakers switch and mix forms during informal conversation, and conclude by raising some questions as to other factors playing a part in linguistic variation and change.

2. Fieldwork background

Firstly, I will outline the background to my fieldwork methodology. I needed to find ways of creating a linguistic environment closely approximating that of natural speech, whereby I could effectively gather tokens of demonstrative usage from individuals within the speech community. Therefore I developed my methodology bearing in mind the need to create a medium with the potential for generating a high occurrence of demonstrative tokens. Moreover, I had to recruit an appropriate sample of informants to participate in the investigation.

2.1 Sample framework

In order to test the appropriateness of the methodological techniques used, I carried out a pilot study using twelve individuals taken from six different age categories. This small-scale study also gave me an opportunity to check the validity of my research question notwithstanding the suitability of the sample framework and whether or not the correct variables were being measured.

The sample comprised both male and female speakers who were 'native' to the Inverurie area. For the purposes of this study, an individual was held to be native if he or she was born in the area or had resided in the locality since the age of seven at the most. As a result, this would bring a mixture of individuals into the foreground, including those whose families have been native to the area for generations, and those who were born in the area (or moved to the area) but have non-native parents.

For the main study I expanded my sample to sixty: five males and females from each of six age-groups. These individuals were recruited mainly using a network of friends and acquaintances attached to a variety of clubs and institutions within the town. In the end my sample comprised individuals from a variety of different backgrounds, thereby increasing the scope for linguistic diversity.

2.2 Data collection

I collected my data by conducting what I would loosely term 'interviews' with self-selected pairs of participants. In reality these were basically informal discussions moving through a range of tasks, some designed to elicit general material, with others more specifically geared towards the elicitation of demonstrative forms. The structure of the interview was as follows:

Attitude questionnaire & word task

For this preliminary element I used the Identification Questionnaire developed by Llamas (1999) in her study of Teesside English. This consisted of fifteen questions which gave the participants the opportunity to voice their opinions on their language and on the area in which they live. Whilst general in nature this provided me with a good corpus of attitudinal data. This led on to a discussion of local words and their usage which I found to be an effective means of accessing informal speech. Participants enjoyed this task as it allowed them to fulfil the role of expert on their own language use.

Visual images
In the next stage of the interview, I used photographs of Inverurie in the past and present to stimulate informal discussion between the participants. By asking them to identify the places and buildings depicted in each photograph, and to describe changes from the present, this increased the scope for demonstrative use. Participants regularly referred to elements in the photograph in a deictic sense as we can see from the following example where Norman (66) is commenting on shop buildings in an old photograph of the town's Market Place:

(i). N: Aye...aye, aat's better. Well if aat's...aat wis a grocer's shop en...aat wis the grocer's shop. But *aat eens* is nae there noo, nor that.

This task concluded with the participants identifying the contents of pictures of animals, foodstuffs and objects photographed from unusual angles. The language of identification and selection used during this process invariably included the use of demonstrative pronouns and determiners as shown in the following example where Aileen (64) is trying to fathom out an aerial view of a pair of wellingtons:

(ii). A: Is it *these rubber things* ye pit on yer feet? (She thinks they are some form of goloshes).

Practical selection
To conclude the interview the final task, which I called 'practical selection', was short and simple in nature but proved to be an effective means by which to collect tokens of demonstrative use. Firstly the participants were shown pictures of different types of spectacles with the request that they indicate their preferences and dislikes. In addition, they were required to match up sports glasses/goggles with their respective sports. This worked well in eliciting demonstrative forms due to the plural status of these items. Here is an example where Russell (21) is trying to identify glasses used for racquet sports and basketball:

(iii). R: I'd say *that ones* or *that ones*...an that...one o *those* would be racquet sports as well I would say.

Secondly, groups of different types of sweet were displayed before the participants who were required to identify the types and select their favourites, as in the following examples from an interview conducted with Mina (87) and Margaret (72):

(iv). Mi: Aat's *thon Werther's*.

(v). Ma: Aat's *aat fruit bonbons*, is it?

This specific elicitation method with its pleasurable content brought the interview to a close.

2.3 Current situation

Currently, I am in the process of sorting the data gathered from the fieldwork phase of my main study. Therefore, for the purposes of this paper I will reflect upon the data gleaned from the pilot study including examples from the recent data, although it has yet to be analysed systematically and conclusively. What I want to present at this stage is an overview of the mechanisms of change which I have noticed over the course of my recent fieldwork investigation. Furthermore, I will raise questions which I hope to address in full when both the quantitative and qualitative analyses of my data have been completed.

3. Binary relationship

Firstly I would like to comment on the binary relationship between the standard and local forms within the speech community. To give an overview of the general differences between age-groups, I have grouped together the number and type of demonstrative utterances for each group as a whole.

Table 1: Distribution of proximal pronoun and determiner forms

Age-group	Pronoun		Determiner	
	this	*these*	*this*	*these*
60 +	0	0	3	0
46 – 59	0	1	3	1
36 – 45	1	2	1	7
26 – 35	0	7	1	6
16 – 25	0	0	0	4
8 - 15	0	0	0	0

These results tell us very little about the use of the proximal demonstrative form within the speech community, as almost half of the participants failed to use *these* or *this* over the course of the interview. However, from what little evidence we have it is interesting to note that the oldest age-group used only the local form *this* as a determiner. As we move down through the age categories we find that the balance of *this* and *these* begins to tip in favour of *these* by the time that we reach those in the middle two age-groups.

Table 2: Distribution of distal pronoun and determiner forms

Age-group	Pronoun				Determiner			
	that	*thon*	*them*	*those*	*that*	*thon*	*them*	*those*
60 +	9	0	1	0	15	3	0	0
46 – 59	6	0	3	0	14	1	2	0
36 – 45	6	0	4	0	5	0	1	0
26 – 35	10	0	16	0	5	0	1	3
16 – 25	6	0	5	2	12	0	0	2
8 - 15	7	0	0	1	1	0	1	5

The distribution of the distal demonstrative forms indicates that there is potentially a major difference in the dropping off point of the local distal form compared with that of the local proximal form. There is a tendency in all age-groups to use *that* and also *them* pronominally: only the youngest two age-groups had speakers using *those* in this situation. However, measuring pronominal use can be problematic in that with an absent referent it is often difficult to distinguish between the singular and plural use of the local forms *this* and *that*. This has placed a great onus upon interpreting the intentions of the participants, which can hardly be relied on as a foolproof method. Therefore, I will turn to the use of determiners, whereby intention is expressed through nominal inflection and other grammatical material. Looking at the oldest age-groups, fifteen out of eighteen and fourteen out of seventeen distal demonstrative forms used were local *that*, whilst the remaining three forms were *thon* in the 60 + age-group, and *thon* and *them* in the 46 – 59 age-group. Interestingly, the use of *thon* was exclusive to these two age-groups whilst standard *those* did not appear in use until the 26 – 35 age-group. In fact, *those* only gained the upper hand in the 8 – 15 age-group with five out of seven instances recorded of the standard form. As a result we can see that even from the sparse evidence of the pilot study, there is a difference in the dropping off points of local *this* and *that*. The local proximal form *this* is less common than distal *that* which is more widespread amongst nearly all the age-groups. On the other hand the use of standard *these* is far more widespread than standard *those* which is confined mainly to the youngest age-groups.

This suspicion was further realised whilst conducting the fieldwork phase of my main study. Generally speaking I have found so far that whilst almost all of the 65 + age-group used the local demonstrative forms exclusively, standard *these* became progressively more prevalent with every younger age-group. Conversely, local *that* was retained in common use by almost all age-groups with the exception of the 12 – 17 and 18 – 25-year-olds who had the tendency to use standard *those* or often the non-standard form *them*.

4. Issues arising:

Whilst these general trends should be of greater significance once the data have been fully analysed, at this stage we are still able to glimpse patterns and draw possible conclusions concerning the participants' linguistic behaviour. It is worth noting that more often than not many speakers tended to switch between standard and local forms over the course of their interview. However, in the oldest age-group, at least seven out of ten spoke only Aberdeenshire Scots throughout. Their style of speech changed very little from the inception through to the close of the interview, give or take a little stylistic movement confined to the dialectal end of the linguistic spectrum. The exceptions to the rule included a former postman who, through his work, was used to speaking to people from all walks of life and admitted that he changed his speech to accommodate his audience. Ally (70) used standard *these* regularly throughout the interview as in the following example taken from the attitude questionnaire where he is discussing the different form of dialect along the Buchan coast:

(i). **A:** Definitely around the Buchan area, Peterhead an all *these*...Cruden Bay an all *these*...the Buchan area.

At this early stage of the interview, Ally's speech is fairly standardised in character even though the circumstances are relaxed and informal. However, when it comes to discussing the photographs we can see his speech sliding across the spectrum in two stages. Firstly, although his speech appears neutral in character, he is using the marked local demonstrative form *this*:

(ii). **A:** So that's all part of the Gordon Arms an en now it's changed again with *this new flats an things* on it now.

The second movement occurs very soon after:

(iii). **A:** Oh, *iss little hoosies* are nae there.

Here, Ally's speech has become more dialectal in character, as he uses the local proximal form in the context of his local dialect.

Therefore, we can begin to see the ways in which participants may style switch within the interview itself. At the other end of the age spectrum, the youngest group showed little style change over the course of the interview. Around eight out of ten spoke a standardised form of Scottish English throughout, regularly using standard demonstrative forms along with non-standard *them* functioning as a determiner. Only two boys regularly mixed standard and local demonstrative forms within their informal speech. Nevertheless, it was mainly the middle age-groups which tended to mix standard and local forms the most; often increasing their local usage when discussing the photographs of Inverurie.

However, many Aberdeenshire Scots speakers in the middle age-groups used local *that* and sometimes *thon* within their narrative, but at the same time used standard *these* as we can see in Alison's case. Despite continuous use of the Aberdeenshire dialect in her everyday speech, Alison (45) mostly used the proximal form *these* rather than *this* alongside local phonological, grammatical and lexical forms:

(iv). **A:** An aa *these* is jist mair or less fit they are now. (Buildings).

(v).   **A:** But…but if ye look at ***these mannies***…

(vi).   **A:** Em…well…***these hooses*** are new doon Keithhaall Road.

(vii).   **A:** Is it one o ***these pots*** aat ye grew straaberries in aat they grew oot the side?

This was particularly striking in contrast to her use of the local distal form *that* which she always preferred to standard *those* in similar circumstances:

(viii).   **A:** That wis…d've bin far yer road, aat wid hiv been one o ***that hooses***.

I have found this pattern time and time again over the course of my fieldwork. It is as if *these* has been accepted into the dialect in a way that *those* has not. Although *this* is still regularly used by many native speakers it is being put under linguistic pressure by *these* which is trying to compete within the same structural niche and succeeding (in many ways like the grey squirrel!) In the narrative of twelve-year-old Scott we can see the assimilation of *these* into the dialect, as he applies the phonological rule whereby initial /ð/ is omitted from grammatical words such as *this, that, thon, the* and *then*. Scott and Nicholas (12) are studying a picture of their school, Inverurie Academy:

(ix).   **N:** That's the front door there. Science is like this side…

Sc: But fit aboot *ese*? The front door's jist over a bit…cos there's the sign sayin…

N: But our science is on the other side.

Here, *these* has effectively become integrated into the dialect end of the spectrum as *ese*.

Nonetheless, a core element in the community still retain the use of *this* although in the following example we find Jim (52) using it immediately after standard *these* in the same sentence:

(x).   **J:** Aye ye see there wis a…there wis a burn came aff aa ***these parks far iss hooses are***…ye ken far the puttin sheddie is…the witch's hat…the Rugby Club…

I cannot give the reason why Jim decided to switch demonstrative use in the middle of this sentence but it is likely to be a subconscious choice; possibly an assertion of the local dialect after using *these* which does seem out of place in this sentence. There are many reasons why people change demonstrative use over the course of their personal narratives.   I have often found that the nature of the subject under discussion along with the demonstrative use of the listener will trigger a change in the middle age-groups especially. Also *these* is often used emphatically by native speakers when they want to use a stronger deixis for semantic reasons.

5. Conclusion

To conclude this paper I would like to raise some other issues relating to change in demonstrative use within the community. Over the course of my fieldwork I have found many instances of dialect-speaking parents who have used a more standardised form of speech towards their children as they grow up, to provide them with what they see as a better chance for their future advancement. Many have admitted not passing on vocabulary which they used when children themselves, and have found that in many circumstances they are diluting elements of their own speech as they mix with individuals who are not native to the area. Whilst age I believe is in many ways a crucial factor influencing demonstrative usage, it is by no means the only variable acting upon the population. There are individuals in every age-group who do not slot neatly into the age-related stereotypes summarised previously. There are young people using local demonstrative forms alongside others who use mostly standard forms. Family, friends, partners and work colleagues all play a part in shaping a person's speech and influencing, often subconsciously, their choice over using local versus standard forms. Whilst one twelve-year-old may be influenced by his dialect-speaking family and friends, another may inadvertently turn his back on the native speech of his parents, moving towards a more neutral Scottish standard to assimilate with his peers. Similarly, one thirty-five-year-old may work and socialise in Aberdeen with colleagues who are not native to the area, and as a result use more standard demonstrative forms in her everyday speech, compared with another who works in the area with other local people.

Therefore, we can see that there are many different factors to be taken into account when unravelling the patterns of demonstrative use within the native population. What is evident is that there is a linguistic change in progress in the Lower Garioch, which I hope to be able to describe and explain in greater detail, once I conclude the analysis of my fieldwork data.

References

Llamas, Carmen 1999. 'A new methodology: data elicitation for social and regional language variation studies' in *Leeds Working Papers in Linguistics and Phonetics.* 7: 95 – 118.

Commercial Scots Translation — A Northern Ireland Perspective

Gavin Falconer[1]

Glotto-Political Background

No sensible linguist charged with the revival of Scots would begin with official documents, the area where the language has been weakest since Lowlanders took the pragmatic decision that the written form of their language at least should converge with Standard English. While there are many sound literary models available from the intervening centuries, those for the language of administration have been limited in number, experimental in nature and highly divergent from each other.

Writing of the recent translation of the report by Holyrood's Education, Culture and Sport Committee into the role of cultural policy in supporting Scots, Gaelic and minority languages, John MacPhail Law said:

[...] this is juist the maist substantive 'offeicial Scots' owerset the muvement's been confrontit wi, an as nae sic a thing haes existit this monie a year, the bit Panel's juist haed ti yoke an see whit *perfervidum ingyne Scotorum* micht dae wi't.[2]

That was not strictly true, since, out of sight of most Scots, a minor revolution in official translation had been under way in Northern Ireland for some years. The reasons behind — and implications of — the fact that such translations achieve a very low profile will be discussed later.

The form of Scots spoken in Ulster (SU) is unique in the resources allocated to it and in having for its promotion a state-funded agency explicitly committed to such prestige projects as a bilingual dictionary, a new standard grammar, spelling standardisation, the deliberate expansion of written forms into official and formal situations and the production of both an SU encyclopaedia and a Bible (Laird 2001: 40). That is all the more surprising since, if one insists on taking SU as "a modern European regional language" (39) implicitly separate from the other Scots dialects[3], one must recognise that it has never been a language of state and has only ever existed in a dialectalised form spoken by a community under the protection of the English Crown. However, under the current polity of an approach to minority languages based on human rights, the easiest way to attract funding is by campaigning for parallel services (usually translations of job advertisements and Government documents) on the basis that the dissemination of official information should not discriminate against someone because of language. In the case of Scots in Northern Ireland, that has meant that the language is being promoted hardest in those areas where it is least well established: formal registers.

Even from the point of view of such a human rights discourse, that tendency

---

[1] Originally this paper was envisaged as a joint one with Ian James Parsley. While the credited writer is the sole author, his views reflect his experience of working for Ultonia, Mr Parsley's translation bureau.

[2] Private e-mail correspondence.

[3] Needless to say, that can hardly have been based on a linguistic assessment.

is unsatisfactory, since the SU version, often written in an unfamiliar orthography and with recondite or invented vocabulary or imported terms from Scottish dialects, will be considerably more difficult for native speakers than the English original, which in many cases is printed alongside. In the case of certain of the most vocal supporters of SU, the symbolism of official use seems almost more important than the fate of the language on the ground. Since the Scots and Irish languages are closely associated with the two main communities in Northern Ireland, translating into both may be an important symbol of parity of esteem. On the other hand, imposing on the state the obligation to use Scots and Irish can also be a marker of "who's winning" in a divided society.

As an alternative, one might suggest a more ecological approach. While stopping short of a "Gaia theory of languages", accepting as a heuristic the apparently nonsensical notion that languages have rights could prove a useful corrective. After all, we already accord rights to listed buildings, one being the right to sensitive modernisation and development.

It is not the intention here to discuss such matters at length, and many would in any case argue that the human rights discourse has never properly been applied, since native speakers are all too often sidelined by professional politicians or enthusiasts. Politicisation has aided the Irish language in Northern Ireland by providing it with a band of motivated activists and placing it, if not at the heart of political debate, then at least in the mainstream. The politicisation of SU has brought rapid progress and an institutional commitment to development in the form of the Ulster-Scots Agency. The danger inherent in politicising an unstandardised non-*Abstand* language is that such development will be warped, for example in the conscious adoption of forms and spellings intended to distance it from the high language, even when possible side-effects of this are divergence from its spoken form and alienation of its users. Another anxiety is that the shadowing of Irish will lead decision-makers to promote Scots in areas unprofitable or even damaging for what is a wholly different language with a different relationship with English. The fact that, for many in Northern Ireland, the enemy of SU is seen as Irish rather than the English which displaced it is a matter of concern.

The translation of official documents into Irish and SU is, like much of public policy in Northern Ireland, a balancing act, and there is limited evidence of love for either in official circles. Even where mediated by the statutory obligations of the European Charter for Regional or Minority Languages, under which Scots has been recognised for Part II and Irish for the more meaningful Part III, language policy often seems to amount to playing off one side against the other. Part of the scepticism about SU among Irish-language activists can be explained by their fear that the demands of their counterparts will prove impossible to fulfil and result in promotion of Irish being "levelled down" so that the two languages are disadvantaged equally.

The growth of official translation into SU, therefore, has its origin not only in the human rights discourse as directly applied to Scots but as a political counterbalance to the application of that discourse to Irish, and some of the commissions received by us have been instigated by a single individual's decision to make an issue out of the fact that a document has been translated into one language without any equivalent translation into the other — a precarious basis both for a business and for language revival. Some of our lengthiest translations have been commissioned on the off-chance of such a complaint arising without any intention of publication. While there are virtually no Irish-speakers in Northern Ireland comparable with those in the *Gaeltachtaí* of the Republic, it is politically important that the traditional Irish-speaking areas of the North in the Sperrins and the Glens of Antrim might well have survived had they been granted the support of Unionist Governments in the same way as similar areas were supported in the Republic. It is also difficult to define a native speaker. In the traditional heartlands of the language in the Republic, there is now full bilingualism by adulthood and growing English influence on the language: for example, in non-phrasal verbs becoming phrasal. In urban areas of the North, many receive the language from parents who have learnt it with varying degrees of accuracy or through immersion teaching in *Gaelscoileanna*. The main benefits of the market for Irish translation are that it exposes speakers and learners to more formal registers, provides employment for an Irish-speaking middle class and bolsters the use of Irish as a language of administration and thus the existence of Irish-speaking workplaces. Benefits in the dissemination of information are probably less than would be achieved by translation aimed at the Cantonese community across Northern Ireland or even at Portuguese *Gastarbeiter* in Tyrone. Human rights are therefore being promoted largely at the level of enabling the exercise of choice.

The benefits to SU are perhaps more limited than for Irish, since the former is not used as a language of administration, not even in the Ulster-Scots Language Society, the Ulster-Scots Heritage Council or the Ulster-Scots Agency, though the last named body has translated minutes of its board meetings into a form of Scots, and Stormont Ulster-Scots Association has also had its constitution translated. Such tokenist or symbolic use is not all that different from the use of Irish in the constitution and official nomenclature of the Republic.

One obvious reason for the growth in Scots translation suggested by the above is that very few of those involved in the generation of official documents could produce them in Scots independently. Indeed, even among those who can speak Scots, many would prefer the opportunity to disentangle a dialectalised language from the high variety on paper before using it. In official registers, that is all the more understandable. However, the use of written Scots as a mediator for spoken Scots is not the focus of this paper.

For the translator, the main benefit of involvement in Scots translation in Northern Ireland is that it enables the achievement of a high level of competence in the language. The fact that the learning curve involved has been traversed in public is perhaps slightly unfortunate, but even Ultonia's earliest and least worthy translations were without the admixture of politically induced errors so typical of some written varieties of SU. The attendant steps towards the development of an official register may well go on to bear fruit, but its impact is limited at present, since so little has been done to encourage use of the language or literacy in it at any level. "Literacy" in this case should be understood not as the basic ability to write but as an awareness of the history and conventions of traditional Scots and pan-dialectal spelling.

The Translator's Dilemmas

The fact that Scots has been so dependent on literature has done nothing for its standardisation and may well have encouraged divergent or unique usages and spellings in the context of literary *tours de force*, perhaps the most obvious examples being modern writers of Scots-influenced English such as Tom Leonard. Official use, on the other hand, foregrounds communicative accuracy, and some steps at least towards standardisation are therefore desirable. In the context of SU, the burden falls on the translator.

The phases of Scots spelling relevant to the modern writer could be roughly divided into the following phases, beginning in the late Middle Scots period:

- Un-anglicised Scots (roughly speaking before 1560), where native conventions were applied and understood as inextricable parts of general literacy;
- (after a period of convergence in the seventeenth century) minimally differentiated Scots, such as that written by William Hamilton of Gilbertfield in his version of *The Wallace* and moderately differentiated Scots, such as that written by Ramsay and Burns, largely limited to literary registers and typified by the intermittent, symbolic use of Scots forms to remind Scots-speaking readers literate in English that texts were intended to be realised as Scots;
- maximally differentiated Scots, such as that promoted by the Makars' Club style sheet of 1947, where the intention is to portray the language mimetically, marking all relevant Scots forms not realised automatically by speakers of Standard Scottish English.

Although it is of course right to connect the above phases with external political factors such as the growth of nationalism, it is also true that the rise of maximally differentiated Scots is connected with the decline in knowledge of the language and the need for its written form to convey more information about the intended pronunciation. Indeed, some observers would postulate another stage, where impoverished varieties of "urban Scots" or Scots-influenced English are written in a form intended to be mimetic not of pronunciation as divergent from Standard Scottish English but of *accent* and the problems posed by "strong" accents to communication.

The fact that Scots is an unstandardised minority language transfers the philosophical charge of deciding what spelling system to use from the shoulders of the populace and onto those of the individual user. For a commercial translator dealing with Government documents in Northern Ireland, the dominant orthographic philosophy must be maximal differentiation, both because the *raison d'être* behind the commission is that Scots is a language to which the human rights discourse is applied and because, although all varieties of Northern Ireland English are influenced in some way by Scots, knowledge of the traditional language and its literary manifestations is at a low level[4].

---

[4] A map of SU areas is provided in Robinson (1997). While both of Northern Ireland's two major conurbations were at least partially Scots-speaking in the past, neither has been for many years, though the dialect of Derry may be more Scots than that of Belfast. The fractured school system, with selection on the basis of academic achievement, religion, and often gender, may have had a levelling inuence on dialects. Its expense has also kept the university sector small, meaning that many students go to Britain or the Irish Republic to study, the latter of whose English departments do not automatically offer Scots.

A second and related dilemma confronts the translator insofar as the reformed orthographies of maximally differentiated Scots fall into two camps: those which seek to use a traditional spelling system based ultimately on that of late Middle Scots; and those which recognise that all Scots-speakers are literate in English regardless of their relationship with the written form of their native language, therefore deciding to base their Scots spelling on models intelligible to those used to reading the language of state. Those models are not entirely irreconcilable, since in many cases the fact that maximal differentiation has become necessary precludes the use of forms too similar to English. The main differences are with the representation of vowels, in particular the choice of how to represent [i] and [u].

Our practice as translators has been influenced by the intended audience. For example, when we translated Stephen Hall's *Giant's Causeway* into Scots, we used spelling conventions much closer to English than otherwise, even including the quite properly stigmatised apostrophes. In the translation of official documents, however, we prefer native Scots spellings, even where we feel they might be confusing for those not used to traditional Scots. The reason for the divergence in practice was that we felt the mass market required accessible Scots[5], while the official documents would have only a limited audience. Doubtless there are those in both camps who would attack us for our lack of stoic adherence to one system, but flexibility and concern for the intended market are entirely appropriate concerns for commercial translators; and, in that they tailor Scots to its target audience, may prove beneficial for the language.

Another concern is that, as far as possible, a pan-dialectal form of Scots be adopted. *Statutory Instrument 1999 No. 859 The North/South Co-operation (Implementation Bodies) (Northern Ireland) Order 1999* says that

"Ullans" is to be understood as the variety of the Scots language traditionally found in parts of Northern Ireland and Donegal.

That means that "Ullans"[6] or SU has been recognised as a form of Scots rather than as an independent language. It therefore seems reasonable to assume that the appropriate form of Scots for official translation would be a register intended to take on the role of high language for all Scots dialects, a function which is of course currently discharged by Standard English. All revived forms of Scots draw on various dialects for their vocabulary, since in some cases, particularly in unfamiliar registers such as official translation, the only alternatives would be the use of an English word or outright invention. On the level of spelling, the main concessions to other dialects are that the <oo> digraph (if the writer chooses to use it at all) is not used in open syllables where Southern Scots would diphthongise the [u], and that Aitken's vowel 7 is represented by <ui>. In the case of the latter, there is in any case divergence between the sub-dialects of SU, as witnessed by such spellings as *abane, abeen* and *abin*, making the <ui> digraph desirable even within Ulster. The fact that some politically motivated activists abuse the separate recognition of SU for bureaucratic purposes under the European Charter for Regional or Minority Languages to claim that it is an independent language is a

---

[5] There were no concessions to English in grammar or vocabulary.

[6] The name "Ullans" is ostensibly an acronym for "Ulster-Scots language in literature and native speech" but must ultimately be derived from a merger of "Ulster" and "Lallans".

cause of concern among those who feel that such secessionism will create an unsustainably small linguistic island. Often one feels that the public's confusion in the matter is being exploited to decry attempts to write Scots in a manner not wholly dictated by the aim of increasing its *Abstand* from English, thus allowing it to take on the mysterious beast that is Irish Gaelic.

Among the pitfalls associated with the writing of reformed Scots is the danger, alluded to above, that the writer's concern to portray it as a language will result in a form which diverges not only from English but from any recognisable form of Scots; a tendency that has arguably reached its apotheosis in "Ullans"[7]. Another hazard is that one concern of reform, regularity, is given excessive emphasis. Gopsill (1989), writing about auxiliary languages, mentions the difference between what he terms schematic or *a priori* languages such as Volapük and naturalistic or *a posteriori* languages such as Interlingua[8]. Although at first sight the parallels between reformed Scots and artificial languages might seem rather tenuous, the aim of both is to unite elements from disparate spoken systems (in the case of Scots, its dialects and genres) into a common idiom.

The lesson of history is that success is decided on a balance of naturalism and utility. While Gopsill may be quite right to point out that Interlingua is, for its target audience in western Europe at least, easier to learn than Esperanto, the latter was the most naturalistic product available at a time when political concerns led to massive efforts backing an auxiliary language. Interlingua's technical superiority was not so great as to outweigh the greater utility enjoyed by its established rival when the two went head to head in the 1950s. In the same way, written sixteenth-century Scots was not so much better tailored to people in Scotland that it became preferable to Standard Southern English, which was associated with a greater number of speakers and printed works and a greater degree of wealth and prestige. The lesson for Scots writers and translators today is that their task is not to reform Scots itself but to mimic best practice. Where there are genuine shared elements between Scots and the written representation of English, such as punctuation and normal use of the apostrophe to mark genitives and language-internal contractions, they should be built on as aids to comprehension. In fact, it is the task of the translator to become absolutely proficient in them, for the aim is to be understood by the reader.

No translator can assume a knowledge of Scots by dint of nationality or class. Crystal (2002: 110) mentions the "genetic fallacy" whereby it is supposed that the learning of a minority language is rendered easier by affiliation to the relevant ethnic group. Speech is a universal human faculty, however, and, while it undoubtedly helps, the mere fact of being from the Lowlands does not confer the ability to speak or write traditional Scots, for the majority of those resident there have Scottish English, or a point on the continuum between Scots and English, as their native idiom. One should be wary, too, of what we shall term the "class fallacy" — the assumption that all working-class people outwith the Highlands speak Scots. That may have been the case 150 years ago, but, as Caroline Macafee

---

[7] Unlike the two Governments in the quote on the previous page, the present writer intends to follow the example in Görlach (2000) by using the word "Ullans" to distinguish modern revivalist writing from the traditional dialect.

[8] See in particular chapters 5 and 6.

(2002: 168) has pointed out, the "voluntary" shift of the middle class to English has been followed by an "involuntary" shift among the rest of the population. The danger of such simplistic ideas in the writing of a non-*Abstand* language is that anything and everything is considered correct. Linguistic accuracy is ignored in favour of facile slogans about the language of the people. If all speech varieties in Lowland Scotland had a significance equal to that of the traditional language of our forebears in unlocking our history and providing us with a positive, civic form of identification for the present, there would be little point in keeping it alive at all. In that such philosophies militate against the movement towards a more limited range of variation in written Scots — which might facilitate wider use — they may be doing the language harm in a measure which outweighs their political usefulness. Certainly they do nothing to disentangle Scots from English and prove that the two are separate languages rather than overlapping, regionally limited registers of the same tongue.

As one might infer from the above, knowledge of Scots is extremely diffuse. Many people will recognise the stereotype that working-class people have the "covert" Scots of syntax and middle-class people the "overt" Scots of vocabulary, the former being passed on organically, the latter continually re-learnt through exposure to literature. Scots are also divided on the basis of their various dialects. The tide went out on the language a long time ago, and what is left is akin to a series of discrete rock pools; not every Scots dialect contains every Scots word, just as not every pool contains every type of sea creature — and some words have vanished entirely from the spoken language. Since the time of MacDiarmid at least it has been accepted that the writing of Scots as a language necessitates drawing on all the resources available and reversing the divisions made possible by decline, be they diachronic, synchronic or sociolinguistic.

For the translator, the lesson is that, as John Donne famously said, "No man is an island entire of itself; every man is a piece of the continent, a part of the main." Scots is alive as a series of dialects, but if we are to promote it as a language, we must turn back the tide to unite them. High tide for Scots means a high register, even if it is limited to literature. Just as English unites today's Scots dialects as a high language to which all are subordinate, so too must the revived language Scots. It is often said that there can be no translation by committee, but at the same time the most successful translators are those who approach their craft with humility and realise that they do not have all the answers. While no grand committee on Scots will ever produce a unanimous report, close co-operation with *the like-minded* can only help. The truth of our experience is that an admixture of Scots vocabulary to a knowledge of Scottish or Northern Ireland English — increasingly passive as one moves down the registers — has not been enough to make good writers of Scots of us; if that has happened, it has been through academic dedication, practice, trial and error — much of it public. At a macro-level, Ian James Parsley and I have benefited enormously through listening to each other and through the e-mailed advice of others.

At a micro-level, the most essential part of such co-operation is that every translator should have an editor. If someone writes a great short story in English which is unfortunately full of illiterate mistakes, there is a fair chance that the publisher will see to it that everything is put right. Indeed, with a world language, that may entail something as simple as running a spell check on the text. With

Scots, the truth is that many publishers will not be able to tell good from bad. In the translator's case, it goes without saying that the client could not produce the work alone; otherwise there would be no commission. Accuracy is therefore wholly dependent on the commercial translation agency. Unless the translator has such generous deadlines that it is possible to lay the work to one side and look over it again with a fresh eye, the help of an editor will be necessary. Moreover, given the unstandardised nature of Scots, it is essential that the editorial relationship is not merely *ad hoc*, for the system used by the translator must be understood if unintended deviation from it is to be noticed.

In Northern Ireland, where knowledge of literary Scots is often limited to Burns, and few people are much interested in the other Scots dialects, even the most meritorious attempt at a pan-dialectal form of the traditional written language can easily be misunderstood as imperfect knowledge of the alleged language "Ullans". For that "political" reason too, an alliance with an editor can prove useful, for in the context of linguistic debate an editor is an immediate ally.

Scots and Machine Translation

The fact that Scots translators have shied away from the use of machine translation may have its origin in the literary slant of the language. It is supposed that Scots is the language of the heart, something which no machine could ever hope to reproduce. In that dialectalised Scots has very often been reserved for intimate topics or identificational purposes while English has become the idiom of formality and neutral communication, that is of course correct, and may be the marker of an idiom functioning as a dialect. As Johann Wolfgang von Goethe said in *Dichtung und Wahrheit, Jede Provinz liebt ihren Dialekt; denn es ist doch eigentlich das Element, in welchem die Seele ihren Atem schöpft.* — "Every province loves its dialect, for it is, after all, the element in which the soul breathes." In the most extreme cases, debates about authentic Scots take on the character of attempts to recapture the idiolect of a single deceased relative, perhaps one of the non-mobile, older rural males, or NORMs, so beloved of linguists as respondents. Sociolinguistically, it is unlikely that Scots fully restored to functional language status would be subject to such concerns. As McClure (2003: 214) says:

> [...] the presupposition that there exists a single, identifiable form which is simply 'Scots', from which other forms are more or less legitimate deviations, is not tenable with reference to either observable linguistic facts or established literary practice. [...] not only Scots but all European languages, in the modern period, have been the medium of imaginative and sometimes extravagant linguistic experimentation.

Another reason for mistrust of the computer is the prevalence of relexified English posing as Scots, a topic outwith the scope of today's paper. However, a computer is merely a tool, and the production of bad literature or bad Scots cannot convincingly be ascribed to the technology used. As Gandhi said, "There are many roads to the same point", and provided we know when to get off, there is no reason why we cannot accept a lift part of the way.

A structural problem for Scots in Northern Ireland is the extremely limited number of people with the kind of literacy in Scots described above. The literary tradition of SU broke down not just once — in the seventeenth century, as in Scotland — but twice, since there was no MacDiarmid figure to lead SU from the decline of the kailyard, and probably not much political appetite for it in the aftermath of partition. Not only are those dedicated to traditional, consistent, pan-dialectal work subject to unwarranted attack, their small number means that it is a physical challenge dealing with all the translations commissioned. As a way of getting round that, we have begun using computers to translate Scots. While we are all only too well aware of the incidence of literature being published in a Scots hardly different from English[9], as long as one holds the end product in mind, there is no reason why machine translation cannot bring dividends in reducing the workload and allowing a greater level of consistency than might be achieved otherwise in an unstandardised language. If we consider the matter objectively, it becomes obvious that there is no language whose syntax is closer to that of English than Scots; it is axiomatic that Scots has not been recognised as a language because of its difference, or *Abstand*, from English, though it can be rendered opaque for English-speakers through lexical and spelling choices. However, if Scots can find a place in registers hitherto reserved for the high language and achieve a reasonable degree of standardisation, or *Ausbau*, recognition of language status, not just in law but by academia, may not be far off. Machine translation, backed up by rigorous editing on paper, can help us do that.

Most of our translations over the past two years were aided by the simple device of the "find and replace" function in MS Word. Lately, however, we have opted for a more comprehensive approach. The reason for the development has been the decision by Ross G. Arthur and myself to translate the *Basic English Bible* into Scots.

The failure to translate the Bible into Scots at the time of the Reformation of 1560 was perhaps the key event which set the language on the path to dialectalisation and decline. Although the Bible is no longer the central text in most people's lives, it is still of profound importance to all western cultures. Translating it into respectable Scots, even a specialised Basic Scots *Spielart*, would provide a model for writers, notably in spelling. Moreover, in Ulster, which disposes over much of the funding for Scots development, the Bible has retained more of its traditional standing. Given the fact that 95% of Scots-speakers are in Scotland, it is not difficult to imagine that a Northern Ireland project to produce a Scots Bible could recoup its outlay in full if it used a form of Scots also acceptable across the water. The Bible is also perfectly suited as a Scots translation project, since the usual problems of dealing with technological development in modern texts are absent.

Honesty dictates our mentioning that one motivation behind producing a Bible in a respectable form of Scots acceptable to both Scotland and Ulster is to head off any Bible produced in "Ullans". The symbolism of such a Bible as the ultimate synthesis of language, religion and politics in Northern Ireland can be inferred from Philip Robinson's pieces in the May 2003 edition of *The Ulster-Scot*. Our concern is with the potential damaging effects on the development of Scots as a language, however, since orthographic divergence inspired primarily by the

---

[9] Such writing is probably more of a problem in Scotland; in Northern Ireland, the problem is one of difference for its own sake.

perceived political need for a language for Ulster Protestants can only divide SU from its parent dialects and alienate users everywhere.

Since knowledge of Scots has coincidentally declined in parallel with a fall-back in religiosity and therefore knowledge of Hebrew and Greek, it is now an optimistic assumption that sufficient numbers of Scots-speakers trained in those languages could be found to complete a Bible translation. Even if that hurdle were cleared, the cost involved in such a mammoth project would be hard to justify given the limited resources available for the promotion of Scots and the many competing demands in its revival. In the absence of a huge commitment in staff, training and resources sustained over decades, it is unlikely that there will be any more Scots translations of the Bible apart from competing and linguistically contradictory versions of the New Testament — however wonderful they may be — and individual books from the Old Testament produced by scholars working alone. Clearly a new approach is necessary.

Although commercial applications leave something to be desired when translating from German to English, for example, with French to English the results are much better[10]. Machine translation from Hebrew to Scots would be an extremely difficult project and would have little utility outside the task in hand. However, translation using English as an auxiliary between other languages has been suggested for the European Union in the context of enlargement. Translating from a form of English to Scots is facilitated by the close genetic relationship of the languages and is of more commercial use given the demand for English-Scots translations and the dearth of linguistic talent in Northern Ireland. Importantly, machine translation moves part of the burden of accuracy from the Scots translator to the translator of the original work. Once the correspondences between English and Scots words have been agreed and checked, there is less need to consult the entirety of the original Hebrew and Greek, since there has been less opportunity to corrupt the meaning through human error.

Using the Bible translation in the Basic English of Charles K. Ogden has had several advantages. It is out of copyright and freely downloadable in electronic form from the Internet. Simplified English differs less from simplified Scots than in the case of organic versions of the two languages, which share a common core. The vocabulary of Basic English is 850 words. Even with some lexical additions for a specialised theme such as religion, it represents a massive reduction in vocabulary on any other version of the Bible, meaning the task of translation has been rendered much easier. It also allows a concentration on grammar (e.g. the northern subject rule), often neglected in favour of lexical virtuosity in Scots translations to date.

Knowledge of Scots is now limited, and the present writer's experience as a language teacher suggests that students can learn no more than a few words per hour. Using a basic but authentic form is as appropriate for those who wish to be evangelical about the *auld leid* as it is for those who wish to be evangelical in the traditional sense and, crucially, will allow working-class speakers of "urban Scots" or Scots-influenced English to re-engage with their heritage. If the consensus were that the Bible produced was not suitable for adults, it could be marketed with

---

[10] A humorous example of word-for-word translation from German into English can be seen in the *Filserbriefe* of the *Süddeutsche Zeitung*.

illustrations for children. Self-evidently, a Scots work based on a computer-assisted translation of a text in Basic English will vary quite substantially from one translated in the traditional manner from Hebrew or Standard English. However, it is extremely unlikely that there will ever be a conventional version, and to argue against our approach is to argue that "Nae breid is better nor bannocks". Like any other language, Scots is a rule-governed system, and if English can accommodate Basic English as a *Spielart*, Scots should be able to accommodate Basic Scots. As long as there is nothing in the text repugnant to the constitution of the language, the question of whether it is peppered with traditional saws or syntax redolent of spoken rather than written language is irrelevant. Indeed, the fact that using a computer heads off the random inclusion of such essentially cosmetic features may render a translation more accurate. We have quite openly taken the attitude of "If it's no wrang, it's richt." In the context of such methods, another advantage is that the Basic English Bible is, at least in Scotland and Ulster, not generally known. Using another translation such as the King James or Good News Bible would run the risk of readers recognising echoes in the Scots version and feeling that they were getting an inferior rip-off of the "real thing".

The process of translation is simple though, in the editing phase, extremely time-consuming. A computer programme of the sort used by academics dealing with corpora is used to produce a list of every lexical item in the text. That is then turned into a correspondence list, and the replacement of individual items is dealt with by the computer[11]. The low number of verbs in Basic English allows the northern subject rule to be applied. That works perfectly with the verb *to be*, since the infinitive and imperative have a different root from that of the finite verb. With the other verbs, it works less well, and editing is necessary after the event. The only other major difficulties are the relatives, which also require human intervention, especially if one intends also to include the Ulster relative *as* for plurals. Despite that, if one limited the northern subject rule to the verb *to be*, an approach which in fact corresponds to Belfast usage, and allowed relatives in *wha* and *whilk*, a version of the Bible could be produced solely by correspondence list.

In practice, we have decided to aim for a linguistically more accurate representation of Scots, including the features mentioned above. Naturally that necessitates a great deal of human intervention, but even here, re-running the programme which produced the lexical list after editing can help spot any spelling errors or inconsistencies unintentionally introduced. Some linguistic choices have been influenced by the exigencies of the translation method used. For example, rather than laboriously change English *put* to *pit*, *pat* or *put(ten)* depending on grammatical context, we have opted for *pit* in all cases, and for the sake of consistency *taen* and *gaen* are also used as the simple past forms. While that may seem low-register to some in Scotland, it has the advantage of being "Sheuch-briggin", since in Ulster, a small dialect area with a disjunctive literary tradition, the natural tendency towards simplification present in all Anglic dialects has been able to progress further, meaning that the more traditional literary forms may have limited currency.

Thus far we have completed the Old Testament up to the Psalms, and we are currently seeking grants from various bodies to help with their publication before

---

[11] This part of the work is carried out by my collaborator, Ross G. Arthur.

moving on to the rest of the Bible. Regardless of whether we complete the task, we feel we have shown the way. Any failings in the product are due, not to the method used, but to the translators; specifically, the present writer. Kay (1993: 184) makes a point about Scots and other non-*Abstand* languages, drawing our attention to the fact that similarity to a dominant neighbour is not necessarily a disadvantage. The degree to which we profit from that closeness, however, depends largely on ourselves.

References

Crystal, D. (2002) *Language Death*. Cambridge: University Press.

Gopsill, F. P. (1989) *International Languages: a matter for Interlingua*. Sheffield: British Interlingua Society.

Görlach, M. (2000) 'Ulster Scots: A Language?' in John M. Kirk and Dónall P. Ó Baoill (eds.), *Language and Politics. Northern Ireland, the Republic of Ireland, and Scotland*. Belfast: Queen's University, 13-32.

Kay, B. (1993) *The Mither Tongue*. Alloway Publishing.

Kloss, Heinz (1978) *Die Entwicklung neuer germanischer Kultursprachen seit 1800*, 2nd. edn. Düsseldorf: Schwann.

Lord Laird of Artigarvan (2001) 'Language policy and *Tha Boord o Ulstèr-Scotch*' in John M. Kirk and Dónall P. Ó Baoill (eds.), *Linguistic Politics. Language Policies for Northern Ireland, the Republic of Ireland, and Scotland*. Belfast: Queen's University, 37-41.

Macafee, C. (2001) 'Scots: hauf empty or hauf fu?' in John M. Kirk and Dónall P. Ó Baoill (eds.), *Linguistic Politics. Language Policies for Northern Ireland, the Republic of Ireland, and Scotland*. Belfast: Queen's University, 159-68.

Macafee, C. (2002) 'Auld Plain Scottis and the Pre-emptive Staunardisation o Inglis' in John M. Kirk and Dónall P. Ó Baoill (eds.), *Language Planning and Education: Linguistic Issues in Northern Ireland, the Republic of Ireland, and Scotland*. Belfast: Queen's University, 165-174.

McClure, J. D. (2003) 'The Language of Modern Scots Poetry' in Corbett, J. *et al.* (eds.) *The Edinburgh Companion to Scots*. Edinburgh: University Press.

Robinson, P. (1997) *Ulster-Scots: a grammar of the traditional written and spoken language*. Belfast: Ullans Press.

The Greig-Duncan Folk Song Collection and the 'Voice of the People'

Colin Milton

In the opening years of the twentieth century, Gavin Greig, dominie at Whitehill Public School, New Deer in Aberdeenshire, was becoming increasingly aware of the formidable extent and nature of the task he had undertaken in 1902 for the New Spalding Club, one of these local historical publishing societies common at the time, which had commissioned him to investigate the possibility of producing a volume of 'the popular music of the district, embracing the sweet, simple airs wedded to song, and the peculiar dance music.'[1]

Greig was to discover in the course of the next twelve years (he died in August 1914) that neither the airs nor the songs wedded to them were necessarily either 'sweet' or 'simple'. Indeed he came to believe that the 'popular', still largely oral, song culture of the North-East was in many ways more complex and comprehensive than the more literary and bookish tradition conventionally identified as 'Scottish song': by 1905, three years into the Spalding Club project, he had realised that, in his own words, 'folk-song has been able to deal with many situations that literary song would hardly dare to touch; with the result that the humbler minstrelsy covers a vastly wider area of human experience.'[2] All human life is there ...

In the published version of the Presidential address he delivered to the Buchan Field Club in December 1905, Greig reflected wryly on what his agreement to investigate the 'sweet simple airs wedded to song' had led him into, and offered a tongue-in-cheek warning to folk-song enthusiasts who might be tempted to follow his example:

> We do not wish to alarm people who might think of taking up the subject, but we think it well to warn them that folk song is by no means the innocent simple thing it looks.

Greig had undertaken to investigate the 'popular music of the district', but he very quickly found that the very idea of a song tradition which is indigenous to a particular region is distinctly problematic:

> Though we take a definite area for our proposed survey we must ever carefully avoid the error of supposing that we can assign to it any definite body of native minstrelsy. We do indeed find a number of

---

[1] 'On the 12th December 1902 the Club acted on a suggestion from one of the Queen's Surgeons-General, George Bidie (1830-1913), that the Club consider bringing out a volume of "the popular music of the District, embracing the sweet, simple airs, wedded to song, and the peculiar dance music"' (Ian Olson, 'Gavin Greig' in *The Greig-Duncan Folk Song Collection*, Emily Lyle and Katherine Campbell eds., vol 8, Edinburgh 2002, pp. 531-539, p. 533)

[2] Gavin Greig, *Folk-song of the North-East*, vol 1, Peterhead 1914, p. 127

songs, the words of which are, or appear to be, of local origin; but even the most original of these will likely enough be found to be modeled on older ditties, which in some cases they have supplanted, while not a few have been localised by simply changing a name or an allusion. Still more are the old tunes common property – the fact in their case being more difficult to overlay.

The experience led Greig to what was, for the time, a radical definition of folk-song as simply the body of song current in a particular community at a particular time; instead of starting with assumptions about what is 'authentically' Scots or 'authentically' North-East and creating a canon out of that, he came to feel that the North-East folk-song tradition was, quite simply, the songs — in their entirety — currently sung by the people of the North-East. It does not matter where they originated; the fact that they are current in the area shows that they have been, as it were, naturalised. It is this belief that came to lie behind the collecting practice of Greig, and of his collaborator from 1903, the Rev James Bruce Duncan. Greig described their approach with some eloquence in his Presidential address:

> The collector must in the first instance take just what he finds. He receives everything with an open mind, and goes ahead, quite prepared for developments. They come thick and fast. As his collection grows he discovers more and more identities, always qualified of course by the variations that are inseparable from oral tradition; he discovers endless resemblances, affinities, imitations, echoes, until there is woven around him and his subject a web that threatens to strangle both.[3]

Ironically, only a few years before, in 1899, Greig had contributed a paper to the *Transactions of the Buchan Field Club* on what he had described as 'the two chief songs that our locality has produced' — at this point, he thought that the North-East contribution to the Scottish song tradition was confined to these — John Skinner's 'Tullochgorum' (famously described by Burns as 'the best Scotch song Scotland ever saw') and 'Logie o Buchan' (attributed to George Halkett) . Clearly what he had in mind at this point was the North-East contribution to what might be described as the canon of 'national song', a canon firmly linked with a literary and print song-tradition. The imputed smallness of this contribution is linked with a claim about the specific character of the North-East Scot:

> Let us be frank. We up here are not a lyric lot. North of the Grampians indeed, song has never greatly flourished....The district north of the Grampians, divided by those natural barriers, and by other circumstances, among which may be reckoned dialectic peculiarities, from the rest of lowland Scotland, never seems to have got linked with the southern regions in lyric life and common poetic aspirations and ideals.[4]

---

[3] Gavin Greig, 'Folk Song in Buchan', in Stephen Miller ed., *Gavin Greig: 'the Subject of Folksong'*, Onchan, Isle of Man 2000, pp. 21-98, p. 28

The man who had been convinced that 'up here...song has never greatly flourished' ended up, of course, with a body of material, most of it collected from his own immediate district of Buchan over the decade or so that he was active, which comprised more than three and a half thousand songs and tunes. Perhaps it is just as well that he didn't work in an area where song was in a really flourishing condition....

In 1989, Hamish Henderson contributed a characteristically brief and lucid piece on the song tradition entitled 'The Voice of the People' to the *Sunday Mail's* excellent free partwork series 'The Story of Scotland.' [5] He argued there for the central importance of the Greig-Duncan folksong collection in recording what he called ' the old underground song culture': because of its sheer scale, he argued, the collection is perhaps more fully representative of folk-culture, closer to being indeed fully 'the voice of the people' as a whole, than anything else that survives from the period. 'Underground' is an odd word to use of a large body of songs widely known throughout the North-East; but part of Henderson's point — and one that had already been made by Greig — was that the tradition represented was very different from what might be called the 'above ground' tradition, the published corpus of Scottish 'national song'. This is Greig again offering some testy remarks on the subject in 1910, in an essay on 'The Traditional Minstrelsy of Buchan':

> People have all along taken it for granted that the true minstrelsy of the Scottish people is to be found in the published collections of so-called Scottish song, and that our traditional and unrecorded minstrelsy is, both as to extent and significance, but the negligible fringe of native lyricism. This is largely a delusion. The songs of Ramsay, Burns, Hogg, Tannahill, Scott and Lady Nairne, and the rest, have never been adopted and sung by the Scottish peasantry. The minstrelsy of our peasantry has been just that body of traditional song and ballad which collectors and critics have so largely ignored — vastly greater in extent than book song, and different from it at once as regards words and tunes. Folk song had doubtless been the foundation of book song; but its communal character and fitness have been invaded by the individuality of poets and musicians, whose conscious art, aimed at raising Scottish song to a higher plane, has largely parted company with popular tastes and communal sanctions. [6]

This might almost be Dave Harker denouncing the appropriation of folk expression by élites, with the resultant corruption of folksong into 'fakesong'.

In using the word 'underground', however, Henderson was not just suggesting that the real folksong tradition was 'invisible' in being largely unrepresented in

---

[4] Greig, 'On Two Buchan Songs', Miller pp 1-16, p 2

[5] Hamish Henderson, 'The Voice of the People' in Angus Calder ed., *Alias MacAlias: Writings on Songs, Folk and Literature,* Edinburgh 1992, pp.1-4, p.1

[6] Greig, 'The Traditional Minstrelsy of Buchan', Miller, pp. 123-142, p. 123

print. 'Underground' also suggests simultaneously suppression and resistance, and the idea of a counter-culture, something different from and often opposed to 'official' culture. Forces and impulses, psychological and social, which are suppressed — or at least censored — in official print culture find expression through oral and popular tradition; in the material collected by Greig and Duncan, Henderson found, in the contemporary phrase, the 'return of the repressed.' One is reminded of Grieve's comment in his important 1923 essay 'A Theory of Scots Letters' on the revelatory effects of his encounter with the Scots words and phrases in John Jamieson's early nineteenth-century *Etymological Dictionary of the Scottish Language*. For Grieve at this stage of his creative development, the corpus of Scots as recorded in Jamieson revealed these forces in the Scots psyche which had been repressed by the steady process of anglicisation; the words in Jamieson were somehow both excitingly new and oddly familiar, as if they were putting the poet in touch not only with the Scottish past, but also with submerged elements in his own psyche: 'There are words and phrases in the Vernacular which thrill me with a sense of having been produced as a result of mental processes entirely different from my own and much more powerful. They embody observations of a kind which the modern mind makes with increasing difficulty and weakened effect.'[7]

'Underground' is also related to Henderson's deployment of a construction of recent Scottish cultural history widely held by those influenced by the notion of a twentieth century 'Scottish Renaissance'. In this construction, the cultural situation in nineteenth century, or more specifically Victorian, Scotland, is contrasted with that in the seventeenth and especially the eighteenth century. So for Henderson, all human life was there in the popular culture of Scotland in the years following 1707. The song tradition, for example, encompassed the experience of all classes; and as Ramsay's *Tea-Table Miscellany* in the 1720s and Burns's collaborations with Johnson and Thomson later in the century show, material passed both 'up' and 'down' the social scale and from oral tradition to print and back again. In addition, at this point in its history, the tradition included all aspects of individual experience, in particular the sexual. This dynamic and inclusive contemporary song culture was also firmly anchored in native tradition: as Henderson points out, 'some of the finest collections of the great classical ballads were made at this time'; and collections such as David Herd's *Ancient and Modern Scottish Songs and Ballads* (two volumes, 1776) explicitly link past and present. Such a collection, Henderson continues, as well as linking the historical and the contemporary, also provides 'ample evidence of an exceedingly lively and creative popular culture, which crossed class boundaries, and which displayed a muscular capacity for dealing poetically with the most diverse human moods and conditions.'

In the Victorian age, things were 'startlingly different' — though as always

---

[7] C.M. Grieve, 'A Theory of Scots Letters', in Alan Bold ed., *The Thistle Rises: an Anthology of Poetry and Prose by Hugh MacDiarmid*, London 1984, pp. 125-141, pp. 132-133

with this kind of contrast, there is no real analysis of how one state of cultural affairs could have given rise, in a comparatively short space of time, to its opposite. In Victorian Scotland, Henderson claims, 'The hegemony of the Kirk was more or less absolute and the elements of Scottish life that Burns had glorified in his anarchic cantata 'Love and Liberty' — in Thomas Crawford's words, 'a world-upside-down celebration of energy and instinct' — were well and truly battened down.' For Henderson, the effect on the country's song culture, or at least the version of it that was reflected in print, was disastrous:

> This was an era when many Scots were devoting themselves to Empire-building, and the numerous song-books that were produced became repositories of the 'refined', the mawkishly sentimental and the braggadocio-patriotic, helping to create an image of Scotland outwith our borders that no nation on earth could possible covet. These sad songbooks put into circulation 'cleaned-up' versions, by poets such as Lyle and Tannahill, of the old 'high-kilted' songs that were such a glorious feature of the older, rumbustious Scottish tradition.[8]

There are several things one could say here: most obviously that the circulation in print of 'cleaned-up' versions of racy folk material characterises Henderson's admired eighteenth century at least as much as the Victorian period. Contrasting his own (and contemporary) best practice with the approach of his eighteenth-century predecessors, Greig remarks, justly, about many eighteenth- and nineteenth-century collectors that:

> They wanted songs that could go into printed collections and that would be taken up and sung. The words had to reach a certain standard of merit; and, when they failed to reach that standard, the song had to be set aside, however good the tune might be. Burns, when he found a good tune with indifferent words, would rewrite the verses; but the ordinary collector, not having the necessary literary facility for such an achievement, would have to let the whole song go by the board.'[9]

In contrast 'The worker of today ignores nothing that is traditional. For him the humblest ditty has significance'.

Henderson's suggestion that the change in the song tradition from eighteenth-century freedom to Victorian repression was due to the influence of the Kirk is, again, not very plausible. It implies that religious influence on Scottish society was greater in the nineteenth than in the eighteenth or seventeenth centuries. Perhaps the claim is best seen as a rather desperate attempt to explain certain features of Victorianism in wholly Scottish terms; it involves, after all, that all-purpose Scottish Renaissance explanation for whatever has gone wrong with Scottish life since the Reformation — whether it is the lack of a theatre tradition or the squalor of the Gorbals, the Kirk and Calvin are responsible. But then, oddly,

---

[8] Henderson, 'Voice of the People', *Alias MacAlias*, p 1
[9] Greig, 'Folk Song in Buchan', Miller, p. 123

Henderson goes on to give credit for the 'rediscovery' of the authentic, uncensored song tradition to two men who might be thought to represent just those forces — formal education and established religion — which were the biggest threats to vernacular tradition in general, and in particular to those aspects of it which ran counter to conventional moral and social attitudes. Gavin Greig, after all, was a rural schoolmaster, at Whitehill near New Deer (and had originally intended to become a minister); his collaborator James Bruce Duncan was a minister, of the United Free congregation at Lynturk near Alford. And an important predecessor of Greig and Duncan in exploring the folk traditions of the North-East was another minister, the Rev. Walter Gregor; indeed, in the nineteenth century, clergymen were particularly active in the study and collection of folk materials in both lowland and highland Scotland. Evidently the relations between education, religion and vernacular culture were more complex than is sometimes suggested. In fact the Victorian censoring of 'coarse' traditional material is not a specifically Scottish phenomenon. It is linked with the rise of the idea of 'respectability' — a feature of the cultural climate of the time throughout the UK as a whole — and with that rise came a concomitant disapproval of many traditional occasions, customs and practices. Indeed, so strong was social and sometimes legal pressure in the nineteenth century that even large-scale and long-established popular events were simply suppressed: the most famous case in the mid-century is Bartholomew Fair; held continuously from the time of Henry II, it ended in 1855. And this is the era in which there is a corresponding (and in many ways admirable) concern to create facilities and opportunities for 'rational' and 'responsible' leisure for the lower classes: public libraries, mechanics' institutes, local museums and galleries. Whatever the reasons for the change, there is no doubt that it happened in both Scotland and England; contemporaries like Douglas Jerrold testify to it. In his 1842 essay 'The Ballad Singer' Jerrold recorded that the street-ballad tradition was in eclipse because 'the public ear has now become dainty, fastidious, hypercritical; hence the ballad-singer languishes and dies. Only now and then his pipings are heard.' The change in public taste was reinforced, as A.E. Rodway tartly remarks, by new norms of public order:

> He [the street ballad singer] was almost certainly helped to extinction by the establishment of a regular police force. After 1829 the ballad-monger could be more easily discouraged by prosecutions for mendicity and obstruction.[10]

The fact is that the compilers and editors of the deplorable Victorian collections which Henderson refers to were not in the business of reflecting a national tradition of song, but of *creating* it in accordance with certain ideological assumptions about Scotland and its culture: theirs was a selective and revisionist approach; and their project is aligned, I think, with (for example) the effort to

---

[10] A.E. Rodway, Introduction to Rodway and V.S. de Sola Pinto eds., *The Common Muse: Popular British Ballad Poetry from the 15th to the 20th Century*, Harmondsworth 1965, pp. 11-50, p. 47 (Jerrold's comment is quoted on the same page)

create a shared national culture through a compulsory and standardised education system. They were out to reshape ordinary people rather than to delineate the actual contours of popular culture. It is a project also which can best be understood in a British context: the idea was that there were different 'national song' traditions of Scotland, England, Wales and Ireland, each with its own separate identity, but as a whole helping to illuminate and explain the peculiar strength of Britain as a whole. The idea of the unique strength of Britain was in turn linked with Britain's economic, colonial and imperial dynamism: in the national music of each of the four nations could be found clues to the secret that had allowed this small, cold, wet island (or *islands*, if Ireland was included) to become not only the workshop of the world but also the ruler, direct or indirect, of much of it. It is a project which belongs to the high cultural politics of the time rather than to any real interest in the expressive culture of ordinary people. The old *Oxford Songbooks* almost universally used in schools in my generation reflect this kind of perspective, as do more portentous publications like my splendid six-volume, large format *British Minstrelsie: a Representative Collection of the Songs of the Four Nations*,[11] from the Edwardian era..

But if Henderson does not satisfactorily explain the evolution (or devolution) of the song tradition, he is surely right in relation to the general character of the lowland Scots vernacular tradition: one of its strengths surely is related to the fact that, from the eighteenth century, Scots itself was the language of ordinary people rather than of the élite and that its written forms remained close enough to contemporary speech to share the energy, raciness and dynamism of the spoken word. It was precisely these things that made Victorian (or Victorian-minded) critics uneasy about the vernacular tradition: reviewing Stevenson's 1887 volume of poems in Scots and English, *Underwoods* in the *Atheneum*, Joseph Knight preferred the English poems to his Scots, while conceding that the latter had 'a ripe, broad humour' reflecting the fact that in Scots 'a man may venture upon freedom of expression which is denied the chaster Southern muse.'[12]   Chaucer, Shakespeare, Swift and many others whose Muses were not invariably chaste would have been surprised to learn this. A later critic, J C Smith, in a published version of a 1912 English Association address quoted with approval George Saintsbury's remark that 'Literary Scots at all times…admitted a coarseness of actual language which is rarely paralleled in literary English', adding 'The charge unhappily is just; but you will not expect me to illustrate it.'[13]

For Henderson, then, Greig and Duncan had 'rediscovered' an older and freer

---

[11] *British Minstrelsie: a Representative Collection of the Songs of the Four Nations*, arrangements by John Greig, Joseph Parry, F.W. Bussell, H. Fleetwood Sheppard and W.H. Hopkinson, 6 vols., London.

[12] Joseph Knight, review of R.L. Stevenson, *Underwoods, Atheneum*, 10 September 1887, pp. 333-334, p. 333

[13] J.C. Smith, 'Some Characteristics of Scottish Literature', English Association Leaflet no 22, London 1912

tradition which predated the Victorian bowdlerisation of Scottish folk-song. Though the idea of a 'rediscovery' of something 'underground' has to be treated with care: for the people singing them, this after all *was* the tradition, not what was in the songbooks — for *them* there was nothing hidden about it and they did not have to have it 'restored' to them — but these words are relevant at least to the 'educated' (a word which should always be put in quotation marks). So much is obvious from Greig's own trajectory. For him the scale, nature and complexity of the true song-tradition *was* an astonishing discovery: after all, he had started with the idea that (as he put it in 1898) 'We up here are not a lyric lot', only to realise shortly after his investigations on behalf of the Spalding Club began that there was too much material for one man to collect and certainly far too much for a single volume which would include not only the songs and tunes, but also the 'peculiar dance music' of the region, as the original brief had put it.

Greig himself was, however, aware of the continuing influence on the folk themselves of the kind of pressures on the tradition which Henderson attributes to the Kirk and Victorianism; this was one of things which gave urgency to the task of collecting. At the same time he was (like Henderson) aware of the *value* of the tradition he was encountering, and so determined to maintain proper standards of thoroughness and accuracy in his collecting and transcribing. What Greig says about attitudes to folk song among ordinary country people at the time he began his collecting makes it clear that social pressures were still having an effect (some of Greig's remarks even seem to support Henderson's implication that the common people had become estranged from their own traditions):

> 'The older people have pretty much ceased to sing the folk-songs of their youth, having long been taught to regard them as semi-barbarous compared with modern songs; while the younger generation hardly know the old-time minstrelsy at all'[14]

(the 'modern songs', now often preferred, tend he explains, to be 'songs of more pretension' — a carefully chosen word — 'usually with pianoforte accompaniment'). Economic and demographic changes have weakened the song tradition too, in particular the movement from the mid nineteenth century to larger farms and the corresponding decline in and redistribution of rural population; in particular the reduction in the numbers of a key group in the maintaining of traditional practices, the small independent cultivator, was recorded by Greig as early as 1899 (this is a report of an address and so is *oratio obliqua*):

> One of the most noticeable things in our rural life was the gradual disappearance of the crofter and cottar [this in an area which had at one time been called the 'poor man's country']. This had led to a shrinkage of population and to an alteration in the social centre of gravity...Changes were taking place in our social life. Old customs were getting obsolete, old superstitions were dying, and folklore in general would soon need a professorship to save its secrets from the

---

[14] Grieg, 'Folk Song in Buchan', Miller, p. 28

limbo of forgotten things. With the departure of such things went certain sources of emotional excitation and of poetic motive and inspiration. Their place was being supplied by art more conscious and less local.[15]

Greig excepts 'the farm servant class'; farm workers as a group have 'been least affected by the changes in taste and practice which modern days have brought; and 'the ploughman song can still be heard sung by lusty lungs in the field or by the fireside.' In general, however, since folksongs are 'old fashioned' and 'not art', those older people who know them:

> are slow to believe that anyone — especially a musician — can be interested in [them]; but when they get reassured and well started, they generally become themselves interested in the quest, and will do their best to recall and sing the hits of earlier days, and their memories are wonderfully good, although at times there may occur lacunae in their recollections of the words.[16]

That phrase 'the hits of earlier days' is splendidly revealing of what it was that Greig and Duncan were looking for; their main focus was what would now be called 'ethnological' rather than historical; they were interested in the old ballads of course and in the historical information sometimes contained in them, but their primary interest was in why those which were still being sung had survived; in the significance these songs had *now* for the community which had preserved them. Their methodology was field-work- rather than archive-based and their aim, again in Greig's words, was to 'understand the evolution of Buchan man' on 'the emotional side of his nature'; folksong and similar kinds of traditional expression were crucial in this undertaking because while 'emotion in its ordinary and undisciplined manifestations hardly admits of appraisement…when it receives artistic statement and presentation…we begin to have material for some estimate of the general character of the feelings that now find expression as well as of their range and intensity.' To sum up: 'our main purpose is, in a broad sense, scientific. We want to understand folk song and to read its message. For this end we must, to begin with, collect as large a body of folk-songs as possible, in order that we may have material for generalisation. Then we must see that we have the undiluted article. We must, in collecting, take just what we find, and, in our record, give exactly what we get.'[17]

In fact, though, what collectors are likely to get depends on their own relation to the community they are investigating; whether they are outsiders or insiders and if the latter, their social and occupational position in the community. If the local schoolmaster and the local minister come visiting in search of folk-song, one might think that what they got would be at least heavily edited. But both Greig and Duncan belonged to rural Buchan in the sense that both were born and had most

---

[15] Greig, 'A Lease of Life in Buchan', Miller, pp. 17-20, p. 17
[16] Greig, 'Folk Song in Buchan', Miller, p. 29
[17] ibid., p. 26

of their schooling there and so, though they were scholarly ('scientific') in their approach, they were not 'outsiders'. And Duncan came, of course, from a singing family.

Hamish Henderson remarks in 'The Voice of the People' that 'It was not until 1981 that the massive Greig-Duncan collection began to see the light of day in published form; for years it had lain dormant in a strongroom in the Aberdeen University Library.' [18] In fact the Child Ballads in the collection had been published long before, in 1925 to be exact, under the revealing title *Last Leaves of Traditional Ballad Airs.* [19] *Last Leaves* owed its origins to the fact that during Duncan's last illness in 1917, William Walker, doyen of local ballad scholars and a man who had helped Francis James Child in the indexing of his classic *English and Scottish Popular Ballads*, was asked to review the material which Duncan had selected for a two volume publication, one of Child ballads and the other of more lyrical ballads and of folksongs. Walker, by then in his eighties, was horrified by what he found — because rather than starting as Walker thought they should have, with a clear prescriptive definition of 'folksong', Greig and Duncan had recorded as fully and accurately as they could, the contemporary song-culture of the North-East. As a result, the collection contained a great deal of 'unworthy' material: 'Music Hall ditties, popular street songs, and the multitudinous Slip-Songs of the Ballad-hawker.' Such things, commercial and from printed sources are 'not *of* the people, but were originally prepared *for* the people by a press whose trade it was to supply such, for street and market singers.' Yet Walker had to concede, without however accepting that it made any difference, that the two categories were not absolute because material produced for the people is constantly appropriated and transformed by the people: in Walker's own words, they 'added to, subtracted from or modified the original in many ways' with the result that the songs have 'acquired a *kind* of traditional character'. Such productions are particularly deplorable: with the appearance of legitimate folksong, born of the imagination of the people, they are imposters, bastard progeny, sprung from the shameful union of commercial interest and print technology. The role of the scrupulous folksong scholar is to name and shame such imposters and banish them from the true folk canon: in the indices, says Walker with a kind of satisfied severity, 'I have frequently marked 'Broadside', 'Slip-Song', 'Chapbook', 'Book' or 'Music Hall' anent certain items to indicate that though these may now have become a kind of traditional, they are not *of* the people.' [20]

Greig's attitude to recently arrived material was quite different; he was interested in new additions to the local repertoire as well as what had survived from the recent or remote past, and included in the collection (for instance)

---

[18] Hamish Henderson, 'The Voice of the People', *Alias MacAlias*, p. 1
[19] Alexander Keith ed., *Last Leaves of Traditional Ballads and Ballad Airs*, Aberdeen 1925
[20] quoted in Ian Olson, 'Scottish Traditional Song and the Greig-Duncan Collection: Last Leaves or Last Rites?' in Cairns Craig ed., *The History of Scottish Literature*, vol. IV (Twentieth Century), Aberdeen 1987, pp. 37-48, p. 42

contemporary compositions like the songs of George Bruce Thompson, which were already in wide local circulation. Further, as he stressed, modification and even innovation are central to a living tradition:

> Living folk songs hardly ever appear to be distinctly old. If we were to treat them as original compositions we should be inclined to say, from internal evidence, that they had all been produced within the past century. But we know that they are not original compositions and that the general continuity of folk song has never been broken. The only explanation of the situation is that folk song has always been, in a sense, kept up to date…Even when the old songs were less drastically handled the archaic in them in thought and language, character and incident, came to be revised from time to time; had to be, in fact, if the song was to remain a living and effective instrument of emotional expression.[21]

It is not surprising that Greig was aware of these issues. A product of rural Aberdeenshire (his father was a forester and estate manager at Parkhill, just north of Aberdeen), one might think that his interest in folksong reflected the conservative and slow-changing environment which produced him. However Greig's initial schooling was in the nearest village, Dyce: then a 'brand-new railway village' where the Great Northern and the Formartine and Buchan Railways joined on their way to Aberdeen. The railway was not only a major agent in facilitating cultural transmission and encounters; it was also itself the inspiration for stories, songs and lore — and brought significant changes in the landscape of the North-East (both inner and outer), in life patterns and in material culture. Greig-Duncan records, for instance, the rich legacy of Irish tunes and songs bequeathed to the North-East by the Irish navvies who built the region's railways in the eighteen-fifties and eighteen-sixties.

The readiness of the folk-song tradition to absorb material that was new or which belonged to other 'national' traditions led Greig and Duncan to break with the old-established idea that musical traditions had different and distinctive shapes which reflected the 'ethnic' identity or 'national character' of the people who had created them. The material they collected also indicated how slight a place patriotic sentiment had in local song repertoires, in contrast to its prominence in the print-based and constructed 'national song' tradition of the intelligentsia:

> Patriotism…so strong a note in Scottish song in its widest sense, has in the narrower area of folksong, little place and no prominence. The folksongist is intensely local. It is pretty much his own little district against the world; for he cannot well rise to wide conceptions of any kind. The stream which flows through his native vale has a geographical name which covers its course from source to sea, but ignoring this the rustic gives to the bit with which he is acquainted a

---

[21] Greig, 'Folk Song in Buchan', Miller, p. 36
[22] Greig, 'Folk Song in Buchan', Miller, p. 44

purely local name. His interests and sympathies are all more or less localised, with the result that national sentiment makes no special appeal to him.[22]
Even more striking perhaps, in relation to the usual clichés about the corrosive effect of Calvinism on Scottish culture is the almost complete absence in the folk-song tradition of religious sentiment, or of reference to religious matters at all, except in satiric vein:

> The church and religion as such have practically no place in folk song which indeed in relation to religion as to love is largely pagan. If ecclesiastical matters are to receive attention at its hands they must as a rule come into the arena of local incident lending itself to satirical comment.[23]

In his 'Voice of the People' essay, Henderson had quoted with approval Tom Crawford's characterisation of eighteenth-century Scottish song culture as presenting (and celebrating) 'a world turned upside down'. It is a view which reflects the fact that in the twentieth century, the folk tradition was seen, in substantial part if not wholly, as the expression of counter-cultural attitudes and values. For those involved in the folksong 'revival' in Scotland from the late nineteen-forties, the alternative attitudes and values expressed through the folk-song tradition centered on two spheres; the 'private' sphere of sexuality (though with a strong connection to the public worlds of morality and religion) and the 'public' one of politics (with a strong connection to the world of labour). In the first instance, in the twenties and thirties especially, radical intellectuals linked what they saw as an unusually repressive moral tradition with the legacy of Calvinism and with the distinctive shape of the Scottish reformation generally. Folk song was also thought of as representing the voice of the other in the public sphere of politics: as the voice, though often *avant la lettre*, of the working class. One reason for 'recovering' it, and using it as the basis for current and future creative and performing activity, was to put 'ordinary people' back in touch with a powerful tradition which was 'their own' in contrast to the commercial popular art (especially pop music) which they had been induced to think of as their own. Writers and singers like Hamish Henderson, Matt McGinn, Morris Blythman ('Thurso Berwick') and Ewan McColl thought of themselves as continuing a tradition which gave expression to the experience of the common people in work and leisure, war and peace, struggle and protest. The writing and performing of new songs proceeded alongside the collecting and recording of Scotland's song heritage, both Scots and Gaelic, the aim being to reconnect ordinary people with traditions weakened by political manipulation and by the commercialisation of popular entertainment, thereby bringing into being a song culture capable of reflecting the contemporary lives of ordinary working people. Hamish Henderson in particular believed that the most effective way to create a popular poetry was through song; writing to *The Scotsman* on 13 January 1960, for instance, he said:

---

[23] ibid., p. 54

> ... in the long run it is the folksong revival which offers the best hope
> for a genuine popular poetry, a poetry which, when it gathers strength,
> will make many of the raucous booths of Tin Pan Alley shut up shop.
> Our own poets, in particular, will feel a real thrill of liberation when
> they realize that the primary question facing them is not so much one
> of language as one of idiom; realize, too, that all resources of a folk-
> poetry of unrivalled beauty and power are there at their elbow, to help
> and sustain them ...[24]

Promoting traditional song — and modern compositions taking their inspiration
from that tradition — was a way of attacking the false consciousness spread by
popular commercial culture.

The folk-song revival of the mid-twentieth century had its roots in the situation
immediately after World War II. Politically it was linked with the impulses and
ideals which brought about the Labour election landslide of 1945; culturally, it
was part of the post-war reaction against high modernism in the arts: a movement
which was widely felt to be discredited by its association with the élitist,
authoritarian and anti-democratic impulses which found political expression in
Fascism and Nazism. The folk revival was also aided by the growing interest from
the nineteen-sixties in 'history from below' which encouraged interest in all
aspects of the expressive culture of ordinary people as a way of recovering
testimony from those — women, labouring men, children, travellers and other
'marginal' groups — largely absent from, or represented only indirectly in, the
conventional historical record. For Ewan McColl or for Hamish Henderson,
folksong represented (and represents, since the tradition continues) a source of
values which are not only different from, but antithetical to, those which are
'official', 'bourgeois', 'establishment', 'élite': they are indeed 'the voice of the
people' or of the 'working classes'. The idea that such attitudes — if authentic —
must be, not just different from the 'established' or 'official' one, but *opposed* to
it was rooted in a theoretical perspective which usually combined Marxist and
(broadly) psychoanalytic perspectives: in the Marxist framework, the outlook
expressed by the 'folk' represents their experience, interests and priorities which,
in a class society in which class conflict is the central fact and dynamic, are
inevitably in opposition to those of 'the bourgeoisie.' A key part of the opposition
is, to borrow the second part of Tom Crawford's phrase, the 'celebration of energy
and instinct.' Such experiences and values were denied expression or at best
marginalised in the mainstream culture of Victorian times, though Margaret
Oliphant's well-known 1896 article 'The Anti-Marriage League', which attacks,
among other works, Hardy's *Tess of the D'Urbervilles* and *Jude the Obscure*,
shows how much the cultural climate was changing — and for the worse in the
view of one of the best-known writers of the mid-Victorian period.

The idea that the 'celebration of energy and instinct' is central to folk and

---

[24] Hamish Henderson, letter to the Scotsman, 13th January 1960, reprinted in Alec Finlay
ed., *The Armstrong Nose: Selected Letters of Hamish Henderson*, Edinburgh 1996, p. 96

popular culture is not just a product of the heady combination of Marxian and Freudian ideas in the ideology which animated the post-war folk-revival. The idea that the best of the 'old songs' were those which drew on the energies associated with human sexuality was widespread among those with direct links to the tradition. In 1925, Charles Murray wrote to David Rorie, a fellow contributor to Greig-Duncan, about the latter's review of Keith's *Last Leaves*; he expressed regret that the volume might lack wide appeal because 'If the ballads stick, there will be less chance for the vols. of Folk Song which ought I fancy to be amusing', for 'If they print some of the things I sent to Duncan many years ago it might help the sale for they were "roch" to a degree — we are pretty plain spoken as a race.' [25] Sometimes attitudes were more ambivalent and complicated by gender. Margaret Gillespie, one of James Duncan's elder sisters, was also one of his most prolific informants, providing more than 400 song texts. Through the young carpenters employed by her father (a millwright), she became familiar with songs which she was later rather guarded about. When she moved in her sixties to live with her sons in South Africa, her songs were transcribed by a North-East man, James Brown, who worked as a surveyor there. According to Mrs Gillespie, Brown 'objected to her having to note down any ribald songs' although 'he knew them partly himself and said that they were nothing worse than the majority of the old songs were, that they were not considered worth singing if they hadn't a thread of blue in them as they termed it.'[26] Greig certainly felt that that very many of the substantial number of songs relating to love and desire in the growing collection were characterised by a candour which created problems for 'the modern editor':

> When ..[folk song] deals with love and the relations of the sexes it is, we fear, 'no better than it's ca'd'. Even in songs that do not mean to be naughty [a term borrowed from Music Hall] there is often a frankness of statement, a primitive way of putting things... Long ago songs were sung in the family circle and in mixed companies that an editor nowadays would hesitate to print. We must be careful, however, not to confound a standard of taste with an attitude to morality; and we shall misjudge folk-song if we neglect to apply such an equation as shall get rid of what belongs to time and taste and leave us with the essentials of the problem.[27]

Greig also comments sensibly and tolerantly on the frankness of the comparatively modern body of lyrics which he termed 'ploughman songs' — what are now often termed the 'bothy ballads' — recognising that the attitudes to sex expressed in them are a natural product of the social and economic conditions of farm work at

---

[25] Charles Murray to David Rorie, 21st December 1925, in LO 928, archive collection A12 (David Rorie Collection), Reference and Local Studies Department, Aberdeen Central Library

[26] Margaret Gillespie to James B. Duncan, 4th May 1906; quoted in Elaine Petrie, 'Mrs Margaret Gillespie' in *The Greig-Duncan Folk Song Collection*, vol. 8, pp. 559-564, p. 563

[27] Greig, 'Folk Song in Buchan', Miller, p. 64

the time:

> If love appears in these Ploughman songs it represents little more than the natural and inevitable association of Jock and Meg as lad and lass for the time being. There is in it neither idealism nor chivalry. The roving life which the farm servant class lead colours their love affairs and gives them a complexion all their own. Thrown together for six months or a year the ploughman and the servant girl adopt each other *pro tem* and without prejudice...Social Ishmaelites throughout the generations our farm servants have no public opinion to reckon with, but are a law unto themselves. They have the courage of their practices, and never seem ashamed even when the results of their amours come to light individually, or afterwards in the mass form matter of sinister statistical statement and comment...We simply have to recognise that sexual relations in this particular stratum of life are about as nearly natural as the law will allow them to be, and that sexual love appears in their songs pretty much as it would have done in pagan times.[28]

The idea that the characteristic folk-song attitudes to passion are normal and healthy does however need some qualification. Greig recognised that the songs in the collection which dealt with love and sex very often did so largely from a male point of view and often in a distinctly sexist way; as he delicately puts it, 'More commonly than otherwise, love episodes as narrated in folk-song have an unfortunate ending.' Unexpectedly, he draws his extensive evidence to support the claim not from the tragic old ballads, but mainly from near-contemporary songs, adding that though sometimes the sufferer is male, 'As a rule, it is the woman who is represented as the sufferer' while the man in the case, far from regretting what has happened, boasts about his conquest:

> Situations of this kind, however, are not always taken so very seriously by the delinquents. We have the roving blade: the frank and unabashed pagan, who braves the thing out and does not much mind though his paganism brings him into collision with church discipline. Like Burns he seems to think himself a bit of a hero and offers to tell you all about his escapade.[29]

In this central area of human experience, the nature of the folk song tradition testifies eloquently to the persistence of Henderson's 'underground'; here indeed is the evidence for a counter-culture among the common people. And it is one for which Gavin Greig, highly respected North-East dominie though he was, had more than a sneaking sympathy for the unregenerate attitudes of the folk:

> We have seen how in manner, in method, and in material, it [folk song] serves itself heir to the traditions of an undated past, and how it has kept its course along the lower social levels, ever largely beyond the

---

[28] ibid, p. 72
[29] ibid., p. 64

influences that have made or moulded contemporary art and literature. And just as steadily and surely has it ignored any creation or revision of ethical standards that may, at the call of civilisation or religion, have taken place in the higher strata of life. Even in the moral sphere it continues the ancient traditions and remains essentially pagan.[30]

---

[30] ibid, pp. 64-65

The King o the Black Art: Recording the Stewarts of Blair

Sheila Douglas

Between 1979 and 1985, I recorded the stories and family history of the Stewarts of Blairgowrie for a post-graduate project for Stirling University. I saw the stories and family history as two intertwined parts of the same picture. The Stewarts are one of Scotland's leading tradition-bearing families, and of the travelling people or *luchd siubhal*[1] as Duncan Campbell of Glenlyon knew them. I was not the first to record them, but I was the first to record and study their story repertoire in the context of their family history, and to look at it from historical, psychological and aesthetic perspectives. My first supervisor was the late Professor David Buchan, and I hoped, as he did, that Stirling would establish a folklore department. Of course, it did nothing of the kind; and he departed in the early 1980s to take up the Chair of Folklife Studies at the Memorial University of St John's in Newfoundland, although I never lost touch with him up to his premature and tragic death. Thereafter, my supervisor was Dr Emily Lyle, with whom I have since also worked on the editorial team of the Greig-Duncan Folksong Collection. Thus I have had the benefit of having the guidance and help of two of the greatest folklore scholars of the twentieth century, and I still work "to study deserving."

The recordings I made were the root and foundation of the project and the. experience of making them proved to be a steep learning curve, which taught me things I have since tried to pass on to others. I also had the valuable help and support of other folklorists, including the late Dr Hamish Henderson and the late Dr Kenneth Goldstein. Hamish had recorded the Stewarts earlier and was an authority on the culture of the travellers. From him I learned a lot about how to go about things, and especially about having respect for my informants, from what I had observed in his own dealings with people he had recorded and particularly the travelling people like the Stewarts.

In particular I followed his practice of being a participant observer in the situation, often recording my friends in the course of swapping life experiences as well as songs and stories with them on what were more like social visits, apart from the presence of the tape recorder. I had a certain advantage in that the Stewarts were close friends and were well used to the tape-recorder long before I recorded them. I also lived in the same area as they did, spoke the same language and was involved in the activities of the live folk scene. So it was not quite the same as approaching people I did not know, who had not been recorded before. I can only advise people in that position to establish a rapport and a friendship with their informants, and to have a few practice recording sessions before they start recording in earnest.

Kenneth Goldstein's helpful book entitled A *Handbook for Fieldworkers in Folklore*[2] gives some excellent advice, especially about how to get oneself accepted in the community to which one's informants belong. But fortunately I

---

[1] Gaelic for "the travelling people." See Duncan Campbell's memoirs entitled *Reminiscences and Reflections of an Octogenarian Highlander*, Inverness 1910.

[2] Published by Folklore Associates, Hatboro, Pennsylvania, for the American Folklore Society, 1964.

did not need that, because I was recording people I had known and shared experience with over a long period of time. This had its difficulties, too, for people sometimes don't see the point of telling you things they have told you before (without a tape recorder). They also tend not to explain things they know you already understand, and you have to ask them specifically to do so. I dislike this because it can take away some of the spontaneity with which I like to shape my recording sessions. But I found it certainly a big advantage to know my informants and live in the same community. As long as I was aware of this and had some experience of the wider world, to give me another perspective, I never felt I was being parochial or partial in my attitude. This is the reason that I would strongly recommend would-be oral historians and folklorists to work in their own community at least to begin with before looking further afield.

The methodology which I used for recording the family history, stories and songs of the Stewart family was mostly learned in a crash course from David Buchan at the start of my Ph.D. project. He encouraged and inspired me even when I had only half an idea of what I was doing. He also gave me a reading list that enabled me to acquire some worldwide background knowledge about my subject. Later I was to learn scholarly habits like making footnotes and documenting and editing, from Emily Lyle. I was mad enough to undertake work for my doctorate while teaching full time at Perth Academy. Thus my contact with David was occasional but intensive. He taught me basic rules, such as recording first, then asking questions and drawing conclusions afterwards. That sounds pretty obvious, but I could show you the work of highly respected people who have broken that same, simple obvious rule. This way of working emphasised the importance of making sure my conclusions were based on research done. If I had made my mind up beforehand or accepted assumptions about anything or anybody, this would inevitably have skewed the way I recorded my informants, and more importantly the way I used what I learned from my recordings.

I recorded the Stewarts and their cousin Willie MacPhee almost weekly, in their house or trailer, in my house, or even at events in which we were all participating. For this David Buchan's advice was invaluable. I learned that it is very important in recording people, *not to ask them loaded questions.* Human nature being what it is, people being recorded like to please you and give you what they think you want. I had to pay a great deal of attention to *the way I framed questions*, so that it was not obvious that I was looking for a particular answer. Also I did not reveal any prior knowledge I might have of what I was asking them or any assumptions on which I had based my question. Take the issue of ghosts. I knew that some of my informants believed in ghosts and others did not. Therefore, if I were to ask them if they had any ghost stories to tell, I would have to be careful to put the question in a neutral way. This is so as not to give them any indication that I either believed or did not believe in ghosts, or that I knew or thought that they did. It is important to develop a sense of when you are being told the truth as the informant sees it and when he is making something up just to please you. This is even more difficult to do with people you have known as friends for twenty years or more. One of my favourite opening questions was, "Are there any places around here (or there) that are (said to be) haunted?" Or even, "Do you know any stories about this place or this person?" (Of course, I asked these questions in Scots, as that was the language we normally used for our conversations.) This leaves it completely open as to whether the story they may tell is a supernatural one or some other kind. The important thing I learned is *not to put any pressure on the informant.*

Knowing the Stewarts already, while it created some difficulties, was the biggest advantage I had in recording them, as it allowed me to respect the feelings and beliefs I knew they had and also to avoid mistakes that would have hampered the progress of my research. For example, if I knew one member of the family didn't like one of the others, I never repeated to the one what the other had said to me and vice versa. I also made sure that any event that was organised would include one or the other of them but never both. Kenneth Goldstein, like Hamish Henderson, was a strong believer in having a close and loving relationship with the people he was recording, and his dealings with them were based on affection and respect. This goes rather against the idea of being objective and detached, but I have come to the conclusion that they were right. In this kind of research, it is not necessarily an advantage to be objective, when you are dealing with human beings. Living in the same community, in Perthshire, I was aware of local history and of attitudes to travellers, from the prejudice of the town to the greater tolerance and understanding of the rural community. I was able to talk to other people, both travellers and non-travellers, who knew or had known the Stewarts. I also knew village names and hill names, so did not make mistakes about these. I also knew that travellers did not like having their nicknames made public in any way.

There are many things of which I became aware while recording people, whether it is oral or family history or traditional material such as story and song. Firstly, I noticed *what people chose to give me,* both in the way of information and of tradition. Most told their life story from their own point of view. The stories they told were the ones they liked, the ones they thought would most impress, the ones that were connected with events in their own lives. There are people they did not talk about; there are stories they did not tell. I had to use my own judgement about whether I should ask them about these later. I respected their wishes about what they wanted me to record. I added my own comments and observations about what they gave me, but I felt obliged to make clear that these came from me. I noticed what my informants did not give me, the subjects which they avoided or on which they clammed up, the themes that did not characterise their stories and songs. In recording family history, I would begin by asking a neutral sort of question like, "When were you born?" or "Where did your life start?" This usually started the informant off and I would make a point of not interrupting and not firing a series of other questions, as this interfered with what that person saw as their story. If the informant came to a pause and seemed to be looking for a line to follow, I might ask, "Can you tell me more about ... ?" something or someone they had just mentioned. Or perhaps I might say, "What about ... ?" to find out about a subject or a person that had been suggested by what they had been telling me. I usually left any questions until later, even until another recording session. There is usually very little difficulty in getting older people to talk about their lives, particularly their early lives. The things they remember and the way they talk about them is very revealing, in both a historical and a psychological sense. In my book *The Sang's the Thing*[3] I experienced this over and over again. Also, I found that most people think of themselves as "just ordinary," and never feel they have done anything remarkable. Most of my old singers also claimed that they "couldnae sing" or that they were not really singers (presumably with a capital S). They just loved singing and they loved their songs. Some of them never discovered that this is what made them singers. Telling their life story was very good for their self-esteem.

The Stewarts, like most travellers, were interested in their family tree, and my first recordings were about Belle's and Alec's forebears. They both came from long ancestral lines and large families. This made it possible for me to start to make a family tree. I used this as a basis for building up a picture of how they lived, where they travelled, what work they did to earn their living, how they enjoyed themselves and what part songs and stories played in this. It also gave me a context and a background for these and helped me to understand what insight they gave them into the human condition. My first two tapes are of Belle and Alec recalling or trying to recall their parents, grandparents and great-grandparents, and their brothers and sisters, husbands and wives and children, aunts, uncles and cousins of various degrees. This was quite a difficult thing to do especially about the past, when a family might stretch to fifteen or sixteen or more. For example, Alec's father John was one of a family of nineteen. My third tape was of Belle giving a wonderful account of her life and how songs came out of it at different points. She composed these songs for the family circle, often for Hogmanay, not for public performance or monetary gain. They were reflections or expressions of family life and feelings. They used traditional tunes and they were very much a part of her life. After this, I concentrated on recording the stories, but family history was often woven into this and useful comparisons could be made between their own experience and how the stories reflected this or related to it. For example, the title story, *The King o the Black Art*, was all about survival and illustrated the history of the Scottish travellers very vividly and pertinently. Burker stories, such as the one which follows this paper, were of particular interest to me because they showed very clearly the link between the way the travellers lived and the stories they told.

An advantage of knowing my informants so intimately was that we spoke *the same language*. This enabled me to transcribe my tapes in the Scots tongue my informants used, without "correcting" or anglicising it. I was less prone to misunderstand words pronounced as Scots and understood local references better. I became aware of this when I found in someone else's transcription a story title rendered as "Three for a Pot," which should have been "The Three Fittit Pot," the word "fittit" being pronounced "firrit" by the storyteller. I had been in the places they mentioned by name and even had experienced "the berry time" and other work and activities that went on in our area. This meant that I avoided mistakes such as were made in transcribing recordings in *Till Doomsday in the Afternoon*[4] by the late Ewan MacColl and Peggy Seeger. They generously showed me the manuscript of that book before it was published, when I visited them in London at their invitation. Whether or not they were aware of the mistakes I never discovered, but I do not imagine that either of them had the time to do the tedious work of transcription, and presume it was done by someone else. The fact that, like my

---

[3] Edinburgh (Polygon) 1992.
[4] Manchester University Press 1986.

informants, I understood and used Scots, made my storytellers talk about their lives and tell the stories more naturally. For a stranger, they would have modified their Scots. In fact Belle Stewart was so used to doing this that she often followed a Scots word or phrase with an English equivalent. She was always aware that she was recording not only for people who spoke Scots. Like most Scots she knew instinctively when to modify it and when to give it full rein, and spoke on the same sliding scale as the rest of us, although in her case the scale was more extended. I found on analysis that my storytellers used Scots, English, Gaelic, archaic, poetic, biblical and formulaic language and slang, in combinations that were unlike those of non-travellers.

Rather from necessity than choice, I used a small recorder and microphone, which had the advantage of not intimidating my informants. It was a small cheap machine, all I could afford at the time. I have never understood why Stirling University did not provide me with something better from their state-of-the-art Audio-Visual department. They did, however, send a member of their staff with a video camera when I reached that stage of my project that required my informants to be recorded on video. It was not possible at that time to get a cassette recorder that was as good as or better than the reel-to-reel Uher used by the School of Scottish Studies. Now of course you can use a tiny Mini-Disc Recorder and get excellent reproduction. Three out of four of my informants were used to microphones anyway, and the fourth provided me with a very good demonstration of what happens when someone arrives to record him with a big Uher and a mike on a stand. The storyteller really felt he had to impress this person, who did what I never did: he asked my informant for a story that was not the one he had decided to tell. I always started a story recording session with, "Well, So-and-So, have you got a story for me tonight?" This gave him the choice of what *he* wanted to tell. But on this occasion, my informant, who always did his best to please, combined the two stories and ruined both.

One disastrous recording session in the early 1980s sticks in my mind, most of which was my fault. I had arranged to go to Belle and Alec's daughter Cathie's house to record songs from Belle, Sheila and Cathie. It was fixed for a Sunday afternoon and I promised to come early. I should have known better, but I had my Sunday dinner before I went to Blairgowrie. When I got there I had to accept Cathie's hospitality, which took the form of another full Sunday dinner and numerous drinks. By the time I was set to record them, I was suffering from the effects of having eaten and drunk too much. To make matters worse Belle arrived late and very cross because she had just had a quarrel with one of her sons-in-law. She refused to sing for me for a completely spurious reason. Then unintentionally I did the only sensible thing I could have done, but which I would never have done if I had not had so much to drink: I burst into tears. As if by magic, Belle's heart softened right away and she sang her entire repertoire, the best I've ever heard her do, into my microphone. Unfortunately I had carelessly placed the microphone on top of the tape recorder, and when I played back the tape it was almost impossible to hear the songs through the terrible buzz, caused by the feed-back.

I learned from David Buchan that it is always desirable to record the family history even of people you are recording for their songs, stories or other material. This provides a context for the rest of the material. I then found that the Stewarts told their family history using the same techniques that they used for their stories.

This gave a shape and a structure to it, which revealed a lot about what they saw as significant. For example, when Belle told me about the tragic MacPhees, she gave it a framework, within which she outlined each of the tragedies briefly, then drew it all together with a comment on the unbelievably hard life these people had. They seemed to be doomed in some way to die in tragic circumstances. This story relates to the forebears of the Stewarts' cousin the late Willie MacPhee, whose life and repertoire of songs and stories I have been commissioned to draw together in a book. Belle's story, and the fact that Willie went to more family funerals than anyone I know, will, as it were, light up the dark side of Willie's life. There are still tragic deaths taking place among the MacPhees. I recently learned from his step-daughter Cathie, whom he brought up from childhood, that one of the reasons he was so highly respected, not only in his family but among other travellers, was because he had lived so long. Cathie's brother Isaac, who travelled and piped with Willie "up the glens," also told me that he stood no nonsense from anyone, stamped his authority on all those around him and was feared for his "strong left hook."

I never had any difficulty recording the Stewarts. They had a strong sense of being tradition bearers, partly encouraged by those who had recorded them before I did, but mostly from their family. The trickiest subject I ever recorded was my own father! Knowing him all my life, I did not think he would take part in anything that meant having his words recorded. He never liked to be the centre of attention. Also, he thought he had told me everything about his life already. I managed to persuade him to say everything he had said before, starting with the day he was born. It actually worked very well and he even told me things he had *never* told me before, because going over it all again brought other things to mind. This also worked with regard to the Stewarts. Also the fact that I saw them on a frequent and regular basis, talked with them on the phone or met up with them at events, meant that I was constantly updating and adding to my information. For example, the travellers have a strong sense of kinship, which is illustrated by their love of songs and stories about parents and children or brothers and sisters. This is connected not only to the old Highland way of life and the clan system, but has a wider and more ancient link with the idea of the family in human history. Learning in this way about the human condition, to me, is the ultimate purpose of collecting and studying folklore. It is all communicated through the medium of language.

Burkers.

Every story tradition has a genre of tale that is concerned with fear and how to deal with it. It is my opinion that the Burker story became this kind of story for the travellers. This can be illustrated from the stories I recorded from them, some of them from their own family history. There is no better way of showing that the link between the lives the travellers led and the stories they told is a real one.

In introducing a Burker story, *The Burkers and the Cuddy,* John Stewart explained how travellers felt threatened by the body-snatchers. The trial of Burke and Hare in Edinburgh in 1828 had created fear among the population all over Scotland. "Doctors one time had tae have bodies an these lonely tinks and people that stayed in woods, they were looked down on. Even when two and three went missin an ye went tae the police, the police wouldnae bother. My mother was a wee lassie and there was an aunt o hers caaed the Big Dummy, an ma mother's mother, big Belle Reid, six foot in her stockin feet, which many an auld tinker can tell ye. Ma mither's uncle Rob was wi them... Now the Big Dummy had tae be cairried in a chair because she couldnae walk. He had a Spanish cuddy wi seggets on it... an his tent sticks tied on and their blankets and tins an pans... They were gaun up tae this wood that they kent ... Rob pit up a bow tent and an took the Big Dummy out an let her sit, an kennlet a fire, went for water an pit the kettle prop in."

The family settled down for supper and bed but it was not long before Belle called out a warning. "There's a steejie bingin!" This was the Burker's coach. "They lookit an they could see the shape o the coach and a pair o horses. Noo whit wis a coach and a pair o horses daein up *that* way?" They were so terrified that "Rob trampit oot the fire," broke the wee dog's neck, took the Big Dummy on his back and led the rest of them "doon through the wood tae where there was a toll house." He pleaded with the toll-keeper to give them shelter because, "they're up there wi the machine and we ken it's the doctors." The travellers' terror made them imagine that the bodysnatchers *were* the doctors. The toll-keeper took them in and when "these men wi lum hats and tippets like Dr Crippen came ridin up on horses," he let his dog out and it fought with the Burkers' dogs. He took his gun and asked them to call off their dogs and they wouldn't, because "they were goin tae come off and search the sheds." He shot their dog and they got in the coach and went away. The travellers then returned to their camp and found it "in ribbons. Everything was kickit aboot the place and the cuddy was tied up by the two hind legs tae a branch and its stomach ripped and its puddens amang its feet." They had, however, escaped with their lives, by what seemed like sheer luck.

Willie MacPhee tells the same story because the Big Dummy was his father's aunt. The story is an example of two genres of story, the memorate and the Burker or bodysnatcher story. It is part of family history as well as having the form and function of the ritual story for overcoming the fear that the Burker story came to hold for the travellers. They used the popular fear of the bodysnatchers to help them to deal with the fear of outsiders that travellers had good reason to feel.

Languages other than English in Scottish Newspapers

Roz Smith

"The *Bathgate Blether*? – och, we never read *that*! That's just the local rag - it's full of rubbish!" But where do these same people look if they want to know what hours the sports centre up the road is open at the weekend, or where they can find someone to fix their garden fence? "Sadie, what did you do with this week's *Blether?*"

The local press isn't out of fashion yet. Whether it's the *Morningside Moan* or ra *Govan Gossip*, you could find a solution to your problem in it. The style of presentation and the type of language used differs widely from area to area, but these papers fulfil a social need. They also, obviously, reflect the community they serve, whether it be rural, urban, affluent or deprived (or any combination of these...) Did you know that in Inverurie you have to advertise for a *Person* Friday to do all the odd jobs for your firm? And that's not the only place looking for "handypersons" these days – it's a wonder *The Scotsman* gets away with *its* name!

In this paper, I'm going to look at the press in Scotland, mostly the local press but also some of the larger newspapers, to see what the trends are in the use of English, dialects, and other languages. To consider first of all the distribution of non-standard English, Scots and other languages, it has to be said that there are few surprises. Gaelic is found predominantly in the press of the north and west, including the Western Isles. In Shetland there is a strong influence of Scandinavian vocabulary, which is found to a lesser extent in Orkney too, but doesn't stretch over to the Scottish mainland. Within Aberdeen, Banffshire and contiguous areas (Nairn, Moray and Buchan) the Doric is alive and well, whilst the Glasgow region is hoatchin' with vocabulary comprehensible only to acolytes of Rab C. Nesbitt. Other Scots dialects are found almost everywhere. However there are certain parts of the country where newspapers are almost totally devoid of anything except standard English, and reading them gives no linguistic clue as to the area they represent. The chief ones are Edinburgh, Lanarkshire (Motherwell and Hamilton) and Renfrewshire (Paisley and Greenock). Obviously these are mainly urban areas, and a partial explanation could be that newspapers there attract a better quality of writers who have been trained to use a certain type of "journalese", which is purely standard English. My personal opinion is that these journalists may be younger and consider that any form of Scots is old-fashioned. And, sadly, their own knowledge of it is very limited. On the other hand, their use of so-called "trendy" vocabulary is not at all lacking. (I'll come back to that point later on.)

Titles of newspapers don't change much over the decades, for obvious reasons. They require continuity and an established, well-known identity. So there is the somewhere-or-other *Gazette*, the *Courier*, the *Journal*, and even the *Herald*. These are old-fashioned words, rarely used for other purposes now, and in all probability many of their readers won't be sure of their original meaning. (It doesn't matter anyway.) New publications avoid the pitfalls just mentioned. So, for example, *The Hebridean*, launched in April 2003, is unisex and doesn't use any word at all for "newspaper". Standard English is the language used for newspaper names in Scotland, with the exception of those in Gaelic-speaking areas. So in the Uists and Benbecula there's *Am Pàipear* and in Barra they have *Guth Bharraidh*, commonly known as the "*Guth*" (pronounced "goo"). The more widely distributed *West Highland Free Press* still maintains its tradition of using both English and Gaelic in its heading, as the sub-heading is *An Tìr, An Cànan 'sna Daoine*. The Hebridean has copied this idea and uses *An t-Eileanaich* as its sub-heading, whilst *Am Pàipear* proclaims with its sub-heading that it gathers *Naidheachdan ionadail bhon Choimhearsnachd* ('local news from the community').

Bilingual page-headings are also used in the *West Highland Free Press*, even though many of these pages have no further Gaelic in them. So we have *naidheachdan*/news, *measgachadh*/miscellany, *beachd*/comment and *spors*/sport. I haven't seen any other papers that do this; and I'd be interested to hear if I've overlooked any. As well as this, there are headings for certain special Gaelic-language sections of the newspaper. One example is *Litir do Luchd-Ionnsachaidh* (*le Ruairidh MacIlleathain*). This is the all-Gaelic text for Roddy Maclean's "Letter to Gaelic Learners", a weekly programme on BBC Radio nan Gaidheal. Other examples are *Criomagan* ('Snippets'), a miscellany in English of village news and "*Deanamh a' Leighis*/Making the Cure", an English-language column on Gaelic medical tradition by Mary Beith. So within the same newspaper there seem to be a variety of reasons for using Gaelic, from window-dressing, i.e. Gaelic for the sake of appearance, to whole Gaelic articles supplying interesting information.

Before continuing to highlight the use of Gaelic in other papers in Scotland, I'd like to talk a bit about advertising. The first few months of this year have encompassed the war in Iraq, the Scottish elections and, of course, Easter. Advertising is big business nowadays, and it does reflect current events. The elections gave rise to a rash of Gaelic, as the parties tried to outdo each other in their campaigns in northern and western Scotland. But they all united with the major official Gaelic bodies to put a large bilingual advert on the front page of *The Oban Times* on 24 April: "*Tagh a'Ghàidhlig* / Elect Gaelic. *Dean cinnteach gun toir na tagraichean a thagas tu taic dhan Ghàidhlig. Cleachd do bhòtaichean air 1 Ceitean 2003!* / Make sure your preferred candidates support Gaelic. Use your votes on 1st May 2003!" On an individual basis, a few political parties used a bilingual name in the press, not only in the papers sold in the Western Isles but as far south as Kintyre, where Gaelic is a rarity, in the *Campbeltown Courier*. Examples are "*Am Pàrtaidh Dhuthchall*/The Rural Party" and "*Pàrtaidh Sòisealach Alba*/Scottish Socialist Party"; and you could vote for Alasdair M., "*An Duine Ceart*".

Where advertising for posts in local government and other large companies is concerned, the only monolingual Gaelic ones are deliberate, so that they get candidates totally familiar with the language. Thus there is a Gaelic-only advert in *The Inverness Courier* for a post in *Comunn na Gàidhlig* (*Comann* [sic] *nam Pàrant - Nàiseanta*), where the job involves liaising between parents with children in Gaelic-medium schools and the education authorities. And another Gaelic-only advert appears in the *West Highland Free Press* for a post with *Iomairt Cholm Cille* / *Columba Initiative* for someone to help set up joint projects between Celtic Scotland and Ireland in various cultural spheres.

Bilingual adverts are run when employers hope that they will get someone with a certain knowledge of Gaelic but still want to keep their options open. So the *Comhairle nan Eilean Siar* ('Western Isles Council), which, by the way, always uses its Gaelic title, is advertising in the *Stornoway Gazette* for a Pre-3 Project Officer to develop Gaelic day care services. And in the *Campbeltown Courier* there is a bilingual advert for New Drama Auditions for adult and child actors for a new children's fantasy drama to be filmed in the Western Isles this summer.

Apart from this type of advertising, mention should be made of the fact that various bodies use bilingual titles in everyday life, such as Skye and Lochalsh Enterprise / *Iomairt an Eilein Sgitheanach agus Loch Aillse*, or *Bunsgoil Ghàidhlig Ghlaschu*/Glasgow Gaelic Primary School; therefore both titles appear in their advert headings, but the text is in English only. Adverts for courses in education, vocational training and career development are published in varying forms, for example Caithness & Sutherland Enterprise have a notice in *The Northern Times* offering advice to schoolleavers. The only part in Gaelic is the heading, and *Iomairt Ghallaibh & Chataibh* is printed first, right at the top. It's what could be called window-dressing – we in Caithness & Sutherland local government support Gaelic, but we won't make any effort to use it actively. On the other hand, an advert on the same page of the paper for Sabhal Mòr Ostaig is half in Gaelic and half in English: the headings, address, name and description of the college are in Gaelic, as is the title of the course they are offering: *An Cùrsa Inntrigidh*, but the course content is given in English, as it's a computerised distance learning course in beginners' Gaelic.

The use of any form of the Scots language in advertising is much rarer than Gaelic and only appears in special cases, such as where there is no real equivalent vocabulary in English, or where the advertisers see it as the norm. A couple of examples of the former are seen in the *Turriff Advertiser*: A Coffee/*Buttery* morning in aid of Arthritis Care, and a Farm *Roup* at Southend, Turriff, where one of the items being auctioned is a *cheese-chessel* ('cheese-press'). In the case of *Dry-Stane Dyking* (*Stirling Observer*), the builder stated that "nobody ever said 'dry-stone dyking'". The company undertaking "*Harling* Work" (*Aberdeen & District Independent*) said that this was the term their clients knew. On a totally different tack, in *The Galloway News* there is a splendid, and totally isolated, case of Scots being used as a page heading, in which the Entertainment, Arts and Leisure Guide section is called *Gallimaufry* ('miscellany'). Otherwise, in my opinion, it is not considered, so-to-say "correct" to use non-standard English in adverts.

Foreign languages make rare exotic appearances in advertising, mainly in connection with restaurants and food. So I'll just give one example of this, culled from a local Glasgow paper, *The Extra*. In this, La Castellana, a new tapas restaurant, advertises *postres del día* to round off your meal, the meaning made clear to the non-enlightened by the context in which it is found. However, *The Extra* has one really erudite journalist slaving away in its offices: on 20 March 2003 in the most prominent position on the front page are the words *Memento Mori* and a plea for a new war memorial. So Latin is not dead yet!

Reading adverts in the press, or listening to someone talking about them, gets a bit stultifying after a while, so here are some wee English-language gems to brighten up your day.

1. What must you be barking mad not to try? The first *Dogwash* in Scotland, in Kirkcaldy: a new concept in Garage/Forecourt services (*East Fife Mail*).

2. Where is the *17th best* place in Britain to have Afternoon Tea? Delgatie Castle Tearoom (*Turriff Advertiser*).

3. Which Local Council collects garden waste, but exhorts you not to include the following items: bottles, cans, flowerpots or *garden gnomes*? Orkney Islands Council (*The Orcadian*). (If you live there, garden gnomes loom large horticulturally as they don't blow away ...)

Now I'd like to look at entire articles written in languages or dialects other than standard English in the Scottish press. The longest articles are written in Gaelic and there are certain newspapers which publish them as a matter of policy. There aren't any papers that publish Gaelic items on a sporadic basis. Where the Scots language is concerned, there is one paper which has a weekly article in varying dialects. Otherwise Scots appears spattered throughout the press in small quantities, a phrase or a couple of words at a time.

The 2001 census shows that 1.8% of the Scottish population claim to be Gaelic-speaking. In 1991 this figure was 2.3%. Paradoxically, in the same decade the number of long Gaelic articles in the press has increased considerably. This could be because since the advent of the Scottish Parliament there has been a rise in nationalism, on the face of it anyway, and it is not politically correct to sneer at Gaelic or non-standard English. Donald John Maciver writes a long weekly Gaelic article in the *Stornoway Gazette*, Patrick Macaulay writes for the *West Highland Free Press*, and Kate Anna Macleod has begun a column in *The Hebridean*. On the mainland, Roddy Maclean writes *Am Peursa* for *The Inverness Courier*, whilst *The Press and Journal* carries a long column by Angus Macdonald. Further south, whereas *The Herald* has no Gaelic articles whatsoever, *The Scotsman* (twice a week) and *Scotland on Sunday* (every week) carry long Gaelic articles by, amongst others, Catriona Black, Angus Patrick Campbell, Chrissie Dick, Murdo MacLeod and Angus MacPhee. All of the aforementioned journalists write on every topic under the sun, making varied reading for Gaels. *The Oban Times* is alone in producing a weekly Gaelic column, written by Chrissie Dick, with a translation of the most difficult phrases. The column, entitled *Dé tha dol?*, has been on the go for many years, but the addition of a translation is recent. Another Gaelic column in *The Oban Times* is *An cuala sibh seo?*, bringing snippets of local news from the Western Isles.

Moving on to the Scots language and its dialects, as well as non-standard English, the only publication which has a regular article in Scots at the moment is *The Weekly News*. This used to be a Glaswegian publication, but it now purports to be Scotland's *Weekly News*. This change is reflected in its "Little Stories from the Courts", which used to be written in Glaswegian, but which now appears in a variety of dialects, e.g. Glaswegian, Dundonian, and Aberdonian. Here are a couple of quotes to illustrate the different dialects. The first has a north-east flavour: "*The price o' drinks in yon pub is fell scandalous*", and "*Ah'm affy sorry fur ye, bein' merrit oan tae a targe like hur.*" The second is Glaswegian: "*Ah widny like it if MA lumbur wiz chattin' up a' ra dolly-burds*", and "*Haw, whit's a' ra rammy aboot? Ah'll bash ra lyin' gub aff ye!*" So is the third (describing a holiday night out participating in flamenco dancing in Majorca): "*Ye hud a floo'er in yer gub an' yer wallies clatter't oan ra flerr when ra Spanish fella haul't ra stem oot yer mooth!*"

I feel that the reason the press don't publish a lot in the Scots language is that most readers have to make more effort to read it than English. Scots are used to *hearing* it all around them, but reading it is different. Many people even say they can't read it – but if persuaded to read it *aloud*, they will subsequently smile and agree that it's not so hard after all! And plenty newspapers are sympathetic to Scots; for example, *The Herald* prints poetry on Saturdays, and often puts in Scots poems, and even small papers like *The Lennox* (local paper for Dumbarton) have small poems in Scots — just enough for their readers to digest without alienating them. One interesting paper where the Scots language is concerned is *The Sunday Post*, a much maligned publication, which intellectuals say they don't read, but funnily enough seem to know what has been written in it from one week to the next! There is not much Scots in the main part of this paper: from the linguistic point of view, like plenty of Scottish newspapers, it could be a publication from anywhere in England. But the fun section – quizzes, jokes and cartoons – uses Scots a great deal, especially in Oor Wullie and The Broons. The antics of the mischievous Scots laddie and the three-generation family who turn everyday life into a series of minor disasters successfully blend the old-fashioned with the ultra-modern. Out-of-date clothing, such as dungarees and cloth aprons, walrus moustaches and post-war hair-dos combine with mobile phones, satellite TV and the internet to make another daft wee anecdote every week. And the Scots language is an integral part here. So *braw, ower-cauld, cairtie, ken, lassies, shoogle, whaur* and *whit* are just a few words plucked at random from these cartoons. Also, an interesting link between Scots and Gaelic occurs when characters like PC Murdoch use the construction "*An' me/him/her jist after*" in place of the perfect tense: "*Ye near made me drap ma guid pipe... an' me jist efter gluin' it fae the last time ye made me break it!*" This is a case of transposing a construction used in Gaelic into a Scots dialect, although it is not a form natural to conventional English.

To return to the Gaelic language, the use of it in isolated incidences in the press occurs in different circumstances from isolated usage of Scots. In the Scottish Parliament there is bilingual signage, and documents may also be written in English and parallel Gaelic. It is a kind of window-dressing, as, along with other concerned natives, people in prominent positions are terrified that Gaelic will die out completely. Organisations in local government and in business also reflect this worry. The following report has appeared in *The Daily Express* and *The Courier and Advertiser* (North-East Fife edition) amongst other publications. In a bid to give the Gaelic language a boost, Asda stores in Scotland and England are to have bilingual signage, beginning with the Aberdeen area, Elgin and Corby. In Corby (Northamptonshire) over 70% of the population are of Scots descent, and they sell 10 times as much Irn Bru as in a normal English store and twice as much haggis. So they will have *Fàilte gu Asda* and *Toilichte Cuideachadh* ('Always Happy to Help'). The Western Isles Council is referred to 90% of the time as *Comhairle nan Eilean Siar*, its preferred title.

Single Gaelic expressions occur in special cases to emphasis the Celtic nature of the events being reported. So the most common words are *céilidh, fear-an-taighe* and *sgian dubh*, in various spellings, some not too accurate. No other word is used for *céilidh* or *sgian dubh*, whereas *fear-an-taighe* has as its variations within the same newspapers on different dates *M.C.*, *presenter* and even *animateur*. (I do think it has something to so with perceived difficulty of pronunciation.) "Shennachie's Diary" is a regular feature in *The Inverness Courier*, although the origins of the name ("story-teller") are lost to the majority of readers in the mists of time. Other isolated cases of Gaelic are found in the intimations columns of newspapers and in obituaries. A deceased man can be described as the *seanair* ('grandfather') of the family and *gus am bris an latha* is still seen quite a lot at the end of death notices. This has more connotations in Gaelic than its simple English translation "till daybreak". A verse of Gaelic poetry can end the obituary to a departed worthy, or even a whole paragraph of tribute in Gaelic, not necessarily with any translation. An example of this latter appeared in *The Herald* on 22 March 2003, in an appreciation of the late Calum Campbell of North Uist. On a lighter note, what about the *marag* suppers featured in the Glasgow Letter of *The Oban Times*, or, from the same column, *Soirée nan Ileach*? Finally, Gaelic place-names naturally occur in the hill-walking articles in the press, as this is the language used to describe the shape of the countryside, from bens to glens and from burns to corries. Sometimes the Gaelic spellings are correct, but they are often just an approximation and fail to recognise that nouns can have more than one case. Here's one example from *The Herald*: *Beinn a' Ghlo*, in which the Gaelic word *ghlo* translates as "veil" or "hood". But the nominative case would be *glo*.

It is common to slip in *snippets* of Scots, as they are easier to read and most readers can still make an intelligent guess as to their meaning. And Scots is supported by the Scottish Parliament too: witness the opening ceremony in 1999, in which Sheena Wellington sang "A man's a man for a' that". In Spring 2003, a cross-party document was published with the aim of securing the future of Scots as a living language. Its title, in Scots, is *A Statement o' Principles*, but its sub-title sounds much better: *A Road Forrit for the Scots Language in a Multilingual Scotland*. Scots is at its healthiest in the commonest facets of everyday life. Food: the most frequently used Scots word of all is *tatties*. Also common are *neeps* and *rowies*. Favourite parts of the body described in Scots are *heid, gub* and *bahoochie*, and complexions are depicted as *peely-wally*. The weather is regularly called *dreich*, and persons of importance in Scotland are given the epithets *numpty* and *tumshie*. (The Scots language often seems to be saved up for insults.) Verbs describe human actions - *jouk, shoogle, pech* and *clype*. (And there's even a regular gossip column in a large-selling local paper called *The Clype*.) The commonest verb of all depicts something no-one likes: *to flit*. In agricultural areas the word *roup* occurs a lot, a sad sign of the times as farmers sell up. In papers in the west of Scotland a frequent noun is *stramash*, both in urban and rural areas (*The Paisley Gazette* and *The Arran Banner*) — but then there is nothing like a good-going fight to make headlines that sell. And *wally closes* feature in the weekend supplement of *The Herald* with great regularity. None of the aforementioned words comes with an English translation, as it is assumed that they are understood *nae bother*.

All of these words make frequent appearances. However, a large variety of Scots words are stuck in for effect in papers and magazines throughout the country. Although the vocabulary differs from one region to another, it tends to be recognisable even to readers who wouldn't use the expressions themselves, or it can be guessed within the context in which it is presented. What matters most here is the age of the readers concerned. The influence of global English on television is flattening out regional and national differences in language. There are still script-writers around who know plenty of Scots, but is it lost on younger generations? A new children's TV series was launched on terrestrial channels in May 2003. Situated in the fictional Highland village of Balamory, it introduces pre-school children to everyday characters, such as the local policeman, the school bus-driver and the owners of the general store. The teacher's name is Miss Hoolie - is this little irony too subtle for even the parents watching the programme? And I am certain that few children nowadays know what a *hoolie* is. But the older generations *do* know the meaning of this Irish/Scots word (and are probably quite good at having one) ...

The Scots put in papers for effect can burgeon during the reporting of special events. And one of these this year was the 25th anniversary of the TV programme "The Beechgrove Garden". This popular series got wide coverage in print. *The Sunday Post* quotes George Barron calling Princess Diana a *bonnie quine*, and *The Herald* uses the expressions *couthy, glaur* and *ah'm no lookin' fur a fecht*. There is more Scots being put into major publications in Scotland now than a decade ago: then, there really was none in *The Herald, The Scotsman* and *The Sunday Post*. But it's there now. Jack McLean gets a whole column in the Saturday *Herald* to describe his week with language such as *wee, wean, idjit, poky* ('small'), *birl, jouk, peely-wally* and *heedrum-hodrum*. And on 15 March 2003 the section on books entitled "First Word" is given over to an article by Rosemary Goring encouraging Scots to "Lose the chip on our shoulder and think bilingual". She quotes the runaway success of Itchy Coo's *Animal ABC* by Susan Rennie and Karen Sutherland, Itchy Coo being an imprint of B & W publishing launched in 2002. She goes on to talk about "the sheer sensual pleasure we get from the language": *burlin bears wi big bahoochies* and *lowpin llama wi lang lugs*, and the "exhilarating depth of expression it allows us."

The *Scotsman* runs a column by Kirk Elder (a name to keep you guessing). Its ironic nature makes for cheerier reading after looking at reports of the latest political crises at the front of the paper. On 26 March 2003, Kirk Elder talks about precautions citizens can take during the conflict in Iraq: "weird convulsions are necessary in order to drink Nambarrie through a gasmask – the difficulties arise when you attempt to *dunk* your *hecklie*." The *Daily Express* is allowed to show that it is genuinely Scottish (!) by using Scots in its Hickey column, which has an eye-catching pseudo coat-of-arms throwing together Scots flags, castle, armour, scrolls and bottle of ink with quill-pen and the large motto IN GOSSIPUS VERITAS. Its snippets of gossip have Scots words spattered around to good effect. And sometimes, in time-honoured fashion, The *Daily Express* uses Scots as a way of catching the reader's attention at the beginning of an article. An example on 9 March 2003 on the Nicola Barry page is entitled "Drugs in the Granite City": a horror story, and the first paragraph starts:

> "*Jings, crivvens, help ma boab*, Aberdeen has just been voted the wife-swapping, cocaine capital of Scotland. ... I must have been hob-nobbing with the wrong people. The most I was ever offered was a cup o' tea and a greasy *rowie*."

At least The *Daily Express* pays lip-service to the Scots language, whereas its competitor, the *Daily Mail*, doesn't try at all. The only article of substance I've seen recently using Scots was John Macleod's column "Sketch", describing the swearing-in of the new Scottish Parliament last May. And he is just quoting the MSP Rose Byrne: "*Ah believe in equality. We're a' equal. We're a' Jock Tamson's bairns*." And on 11th March, Jeremy Hodges proclaims in his column "Television Mail": in The Inspector Lynley Mysteries, Sharon Small, born in Drumchapel, plays a wee Cockney sparrow to perfection as D.S. *Havers* (noun, Scots, meaning "nonsense"). The feeling that an English translation is necessary is echoed in other publications with a wide distributon, such as The *Courier and Advertiser*, where that couthy Dundee writer Craigie puts a lot of amusing trivia into his column. Here are a couple of examples:

> 1. An explanation of the word *corrie-haundit* or *corrie-fistit*, stating that it originated with the Carr or Kerr clan, who were believed to be mostly left-handed, but not offering the original derivation from the Gaelic word *ceàrr* 'wrong' or 'left'.
> 2. A discussion as to what the one-time children's activity called *hurlie-*

hacket was, stating that it entailed sliding down a hill on a home-made sledge – a *hurl* being a ride in a wheeled vehicle (Chambers dictionary), and *hacket* being Scots for cow, the horns of which beast were used as handlebars to steer the sled.
3. (March 2003 during the conflict in Iraq). A conversation between two elderly women overheard on a local bus taking Fife rural dwellers into Kirkcaldy: "The bus is awfy quiet the day." "Aye, it's because o' this war folk are feart tae traival."

Going on now to newspapers with a smaller circulation, Scots can be used to good effect there too: for example *The Arran Banner* describes a *weel-kent* politician getting out of a car to address a meeting, wearing a *semmit* and a crumpled suit. The same Arran paper makes several refences to the *Chookie* Show, an avian version of Crufts, won in 2002 by an Australian finch. *The Inverurie Gazette* refers to a *girning* Icelandic footballer, who shall remain nameless. And *The Arbroath Herald* has a regular feature printing school and club photos of yesteryear entitled "*D'Ye Mind Lang Syne?...*".

Finally, there are many publications with a policy of carrying no Scots whatsoever. These include *The Buteman, Kintyre News* and *Killin News*. Sad to say, some smaller papers like these are written by English people now living in Scotland whose efforts to include residents of Scots origin have been rebuffed, with apologies offered such as "can't write" or "not educated enough", covering that engrained Scots trait of modesty, indifference or lack of confidence.

The publications of the Northern Isles provide long spells of puzzlement for the uninitiated, as the dialects of Orkney and Shetland are full of vocabulary derived from Norse languages and rarely used elsewhere in Scotland. Orkney provides the link with northern mainland dialects, as can be seen in the following extracts from *The Orcadian* of 27 March 2003. During a search for a stray cat Mary Bichan describes how it "shot into the garage where it vanished behind a *girnel*". And support for the common usage of the word is lent by an advert for the AGM of Orkney Sailing Club, being held in *The Girnel* to discuss the renovation of *The Girnel*. Environmental Concern Orkney has a large advertisement in the same paper for Bag the *Bruck* 2003, Orkney's annual clean-up weekend targeting rubbish on the beaches. (Small publications in the north-eastern mainland have a variation of this word on their agricultural pages: "where there is stock there is *brock* ('waste'). On to *The Shetland Times* now, and in the same vein, the column Northern Outlook by John Coutts has a snippet on 4 April 2003 entitled Early *voar redd-up*: "It was identified that an earlier than usual *voar redd-up* was required in Fetlar. The winter storms have created a much bigger mess on the beaches than usual." Whilst various forms of *redd* ('spring-clean') are used in northern mainland Scotland, *voar* ('spring', the season) would be understood more easily by speakers of Scandinavian languages. A couple of burning issues discussed in the same edition of *The Shetland Times* are possible revision of the Shetland *udal* law and the installation of more *windie-craas*. *Udal* means, roughly speaking "belonging to nobody in particular" (the opposite of "feudal"). "The Crown does not own the seas and seabed around Shetland and Orkney which were and are *udal.*" *Windie-craas* are wind turbines which are covering more and more of the Shetland landscape. As everywhere else, they generate renewable energy and heated discussions. Other more common words taken from the same paper are *peerie* ('small'), *hairst* ('harvest'), *bruck*, fedder ('father'), Car *o' da* Week, *du*, *dus* and *dee* (singular forms of *you, you are* and *your*). Shetland dialect still distinguishes between the singular and plural forms of the second person, and reports in the local press reflect this.

Having moved right on to the fringes of Scotland in this examination of the press, I want now briefly to venture outside the country. Newspapers in Scotland have a cavalier attitude to foreign languages: if they get the orthography correct, that's frequently a matter of luck, and if the meaning is approximately accurate, that's OK too. This may sound a negative attitude to take, but as a linguist, I know that the man in the street's approach to languages hasn't changed over the years. Everyone speaks English anyway, so why bother with other languages? As I've already said, *The Daily Express* Hickey's column is called IN GOSSIPUS VERITAS: when it began in its revamped form in 2002, there was correspondence about the bad grammar and improvements were suggested, none of which was correct Latin. But it's not to be taken seriously anyway, which is more than can be said for *The Arbroath Herald's* page on "Births, Marriages, Deaths and *In Memoriams*". Greek appears correctly in *The Daily Express*, where *hoi polloi* is used as a synonym for ordinary people. (It is often thought of as meaning the exact opposite, the idle rich, probably as a result of how *hoi polloi* sounds when pronounced by someone from Costorphine or Kelvinside.) French is a hit or miss job – as we know there is a linguistic connection with Scots in any case, and the words *douce, ashet* and *tassie* often appear in print. But French vocabulary can be spelled correctly as in "Jessie Kesson was a great *raconteur*" (*The Buteman*) or incorrectly, as in *bon mots* (*The Herald*) or *deja vu* (*The Sunday Post*). Agreements and accents are dismissed out of hand, the latter being a nuisance to find on a keyboard. The meaning and pronunciation can be considerably altered by the omission of accents, but it doesn't matter — you know what we mean anyway! So what about *sma kottbullar* and *smorgasbord*, Swedish meatballs to you, in *The Herald*? Why can't the writer copy *små köttbullar* or *smörgåsbord*? *The Herald* gives a correct version of *moules et frites* ordered in a Bruges restaurant and continues with a shopping trip to the *chocolatier*, for "a simple selection, nothing fancy … As the customer sensed a lack of understanding, he shouted with a clarity of diction worthy of Hercule Poirot: *nae nuts*! It seemed to work".

Most British people have a fairly comfortable, if inaccurate, relationship with French, having been taught it in school. However, German, another "school" language, is a different kettle of fish, since it is perceived as difficult. The orthography frightens learners off for a start. Hence it is largely avoided in print too, with the exception of one word – food again! – which is becoming increasingly fashionable. *Torten*, spelled with a small initial letter and used in the plural, is used in culinary columns as a generic term for any kind of cake originating in a German-speaking country, whereas its original meaning is much narrower and involves pastry in the recipe. *The Daily Express* reports in ungrammatical Spanish on an encounter with a security guard in Dundee: *"Hola, da la bienvenida al Centra da Wellgate!"* The city is trying to make foreign visitors feel more at home. Hickey concludes "I can only imagine he mistook the rakish angle of my trilby for a matador's hat!" *The Sunday Express* reports on a Search and Rescue dog called *Ki*, and goes on to explain that *"Ki* is the Cornish name for dog". And finally several papers made a valiant attempt at Lithuanian on 3 March 2003, prior to Scotland's football match against that country: *Mes istikimi futbolui* ('We love football').

Having investigated it on a fairly wide basis, I don't think as some people do, that the language in local and national newspapers in Scotland is becoming more homogeneous. However, it is changing. Vocabulary is being used in high-quality papers which would have been avoided in serious articles ten or fifteen years ago. The following are examples taken from *The Herald* and *The Scotsman*: *bash* ('party'), *fab*, *sad* ('boring'), *ciggie*, *gollop* ('gulp down'), *blootered* ('intoxicated') and *hairy* ('dangerous'). There might be an excuse for the last word, however, as this particular *hairy* situation involved a man who had his hirsute chest waxed for charity. But the reading public like a mixture of the new and the old, as can be witnessed by the popularity of "Oor Wullie" and "The Broons". Whilst employing old words such as *glaikit, scunnered, rammy* and *gowk*, these cartoon characters enjoy their line-dancing, mobile phones, sunbeds, fake tans and hair mousse. And there can still be misunderstandings: after all *moose* is the Scots for *mouse, is it no, an' no' stuff ye stick oan yer heid!*

New inventions are often met with resistance, due to fear of losing the old and familiar. So the development of Information Technology has been seen as both a help and a hindrance to the survival of different languages. English is what is used globally in this field, so will IT hasten the demise of Gaelic etc.? A report in *The Herald* of 24 May 2003 is optimistic. Both the old Comunn na Gàidhlig and Bord na Gàidhlig, the new agency responsible for the development of Gaelic culture, hope that a deal can be struck with Microsoft to produce a computerised Gaelic dictionary. This would stem Gaelic's slow decline, by improving literacy among the thousands of speakers who can't write or spell the language. Part of the work has already been completed, in order to create the Gaelic glossary used by the Scottish Parliament, and this stamp of official approval will also encourage the growth of the language.

Another recent development is text-messaging. But maybe it's just a convenient continuation of many British people's secret liking of phonetic spelling: it's a bit infra-dig, but it's fun. Remember the 1960s and 70s, with Slade's *"Cum on feel the noize"*? Nowadays there are adverts in the press – here's one from *The Press and Journal* of 21 April 2003: *If UR selling ... get txtin! 4 a fast response entR ur name & adr$. Send ur m$ge to 81800*. And now you can text-message in Gaelic too, as reported in *The Hebridean* (18.04.03), *The Herald* (19.04.03) and *Am Pàipear* (May 03). What about *tapl@* ('tapadh leat), *8ucolrm?* ('an tèid thu còmhla rium?'), *jkyr?* ('dè tha ceàrr?') and *n8* ('a-nochd')? *frs2!*

(*furasda*, 'easy!').

So I think languages other than English are alive and well in the local press in Scotland. They always show up in every type of newspaper in cartoons, where they are used to make fun of some of the daft situations occurring in every walk of life. For example, this spring the press went to town on the controversy in the Uists over whether hedgehogs are pests or not, the £5 bounty for each animal caught and the efforts of official bodies to airlift them to other parts of Britain.